THE TVAREG

D0896645

THE TVAREG

Kenneth and Julie Slavin

Foreword by John Julius Norwich

Photographs by Roger Balsom

GENTRY BOOKS · LONDON

© Quest 4 Limited, 1973
First published November 1973
Galleon paperback edition first published September 1974.
ISBN 0 904 442020

All rights reserved. Without written permission from Gentry Books Limited, this volume, or any part of it, may not be reproduced by any means or in any form.

Published by Gentry Books Limited
15 Tooks Court, London, EC4A ILA
Designed by Brian Roll
Printed by Ebenezer Baylis & Son Limited, Leicester and London

Acknowledgements

We would like to thank the following for their help and co-operation over the last five years:

British Leyland Motor Corporation Ltd.
Harrods' Food Department
The Niger Government
Peninsular and Oriental Steam Navigation Co.

Contents

Illustrations

All photographs by Roger Balsom, unless otherwise stated
The chapter headings illustrate different types of Tuareg jewellery, and were drawn
by Barney Broadbent
The map on pages 132-133 shows the areas inhabited by the Tuareg today
(cartography: David L. Fryer & Co.)

Colour Photographs

Salt being mined at Bilma
Cakes of salt baking in the sun at Tegguiddan-Tessoum

Monochrome Photographs

A typical drum of the nomadic Tuareg

A camel man on the Tassili N'Ajjer proudly shows the jaws of his piebald camel

Introduction

When, six years ago, I settled down to write the introduction to my own book on the Sahara, I pointed out that there were two sorts of travel writing—that of the expert and that of the Innocent Abroad. Mine, based on a single, seven-week journey, thudded squarely into the second category; I feel all the more honoured now to be asked to introduce so palpable an example of the first.

There can be few people in England better qualified to write about the Sahara in general, and the Tuareg in particular, than Ken and Julie Slavin. Separately and together, they have travelled the desert for years; and the mutual sympathy that has grown up between them and the most intriguing of Saharan tribes emerges unmistakably from these pages—nowhere with more impact than in the extraordinary account of the Tuareg celebration of their marriage, with which their book ends. This sympathy alone suffices to make it the most valuable study of the subject in English since Lord Rennell of Rodd's great work of nearly half a century ago, and to give it an importance that the authors' amateur standpoint in no way diminishes. Amateurs they may be, but in the best, truest sense of the word: people who love their subject, and whose love allows them a special insight that no amount of cold scientific investigation can hope to match.

And nowhere is this insight more necessary than in the Sahara; for the Sahara is itself a state of mind. That huge, terrifying world beyond the oases, perfectly silent and perfectly clean—where even time, if it exists at all, leaves no traces of its passage —demands of its inhabitants unconditional surrender and then imposes its own terms. To Europeans, those terms call not only for physical, but for mental and spiritual adjustment as well. If, like the Slavins, they can make it, they will return again and again; if they cannot, they must leave or be destroyed.

Tragically, such destruction now faces many of the inhabitants themselves. The catastrophic drought of recent years suggests that the long-term process of desiccation is accelerating; if so, it may be this, rather than any number of oil-fields or desert lorries that will bring about the end of the Saharan way of life. Nor will there be much hope of cure; no Saharan needs lessons in the implacability of nature. But the desert itself will not change; it will continue to be what it has always been: one of the most beautiful, magical, numinous places of the Earth. I am grateful to the Slavins for having brought it back to me.

John Julius Norwich
Zell-am-See
August 1973

THE
TUAREG

Expedition Log

17th April 1970

Leave Timbuctou early after snatched breakfast, heading E. along northern banks of the Niger river. Weather still windy and pretty warm (108°F. at mid-day). Eastwards of Timbuctou far easier travelling than to the South, without the complications of crossing the river, and we make good headway all morning. Many hippo. bask in river, gazing complacently at dusty, hot and bothered travellers, and reticulated giraffe amidst sparse vegetation of palm trees, spindly thorn bushes and baobab trees – count 37 giraffe during the day including one dead one, huge at ground level. Reach Gao early afternoon. Bustling and interesting market. Buy Tuareg ring of polished crescent-shaped stone set in silver, intricate xylophone made of wood and gourds bound together with leather, some wooden scoops for measuring grain or tobacco, 4 kilos of fresh carrots and even some shrivelled limes. Intrigued by activity beside the river, and by old-fashioned hand-operated petrol pump from which we fill up Landrovers – laboriously! Wind persists, but we set off again to search for a suitable camping place. Punctured tyre, and engine still over-heating. Desolate terrain – inanimate and harsh in this relentless wind. Darkness falls and all the passengers are tired out, though the three septuagenarians are bearing up well. Pull off into narrow wadi with stony floor to cook some food and get to bed. Tempers frayed as we unload the gear. Perhaps an early night is the answer . . .

A good dinner had been eaten, tents pitched, coffee brewed – and the wind had

1

subsided with the sun's setting. It was quiet now, but for the slow sounds of murmured conversation, the meal being cleared and crockery washed. The air had cooled and the pallid light of the moon transformed the hot sand to a blue-white sheen over the desert landscape. During a brief spell of complete tranquillity a shrill cry – almost like that of a bird – pierced the calm, followed by a distant clamour which could be dimly recognized as camels galloping on the horizon. They were approaching the yellow light of our lamp, in which a million moths swooped and spun. Soon the silhouettes of riders became also apparent. There were six of them. At some distance they dismounted and leading their camels they walked forwards with an ambling, unhurried gait, their hands fluttering about their faces, adjusting, formalizing their head-dresses. Once within earshot we could hear laughter amongst them – but who were they? In this remote region who would be passing, and why? Their faces were invisible behind swathes of black material, but for shining, alert eyes that flashed in the lamplight as they came nearer. Unhesitantly they came and greeted us, assessing us and our possessions at a glance – touching the vehicles with reverence. We all shook hands, and sat down together on the cool stones, camels retreating into the shadows. They were young men, tall and erect in their bearing, and even when seated they seemed elegantly proportioned. Each wore an elaborate head-dress of cotton, black voluminous trousers and a loose blue robe embroidered at the neck. They were festooned in leather pouches hung on fine threads of thonging, and suspended from brightly coloured braid across their chests were ornately sheathed swords. Before long they had spotted the wooden xylophone that we had bought in Gao that afternoon and one of them leapt up to play it. Sitting cross-legged before it, he delicately held the two sticks whose ends were padded with leather, and softly began to play, tapping the notes with light strokes. One of his companions came to stand behind him, producing from a deep pocket a small hand-made flute that he put to his lips from beneath his veil, revealing none of his features. Filling the air with music the two young men started to show their skill, the seated one manipulating his instrument with ease, beating the hammers so fast as to make them invisible. Increasing in volume all the time, the rhythm was now building up, while the flute's high and clear notes skipped and faltered – like a frightened gazelle – over those of the tumbling, cascading – sometimes threatening – xylophone.

Not to be outdone, three of the other visiting tribesmen stood up to dance, thumping their sandal-clad feet onto a patch of fine sand, while the fourth clapped his hands and shrieked encouragement. Their dance was downwards from the hips, leaving the upper part of the body for separate expression: arms high, outstretched, curling and waving, eyes narrowed and flashing, and head thrust forwards. Feet were never still, emphatically stamping out the rhythm in subtle sequence, so that the sand rose around them, clouding the atmosphere. The music was changing now, becoming stronger and more violent, the two musicians glorying in the response they were receiving. The dancers seemed tireless, spinning and turning with intoxicated abandon, crouching and leaping into the air, spasmodically uttering bloodcurdling cries. And then the gleam of a sword blade sliced the air, and a mock battle was about to ensue. The other swords were drawn; they clashed and scraped as the fighters stabbed the air, and the music rose and fell, symbolizing the enemy dying. This excited the dancers still more, and they became a kaleidoscope of swirling robes, gleaming steel and pounding feet. The xylophone, the flute, the shrieking and the clapping were casting a strange spell on them and they performed now as though in a trance, oblivious of their actions as they lunged and jerked with their weapons, fencing with the thick air, swaying, lurching, then pivoting around to stamp, hiss and squeal, becoming wilder, and more and more savage. Blood – from where? And more blood, spattered over hands, arms, feet.

The music stopped. The musicians turned anxiously to the dancers, who stood still and proud, lungs heaving, wet with blood and sweat. They replaced their now stained swords, head-dresses and veils awry, and began embracing each other, like the last survivors of a colossal war.

While we rummaged for a First Aid kit, a voice – spluttering with fury – reached us from one of the tents:

'For the thousandth time, will someone make those ignorant goddam monkeys get to hell out of here – we wanna git some sleep!' as though from a far away, unknown planet.

I. Approach

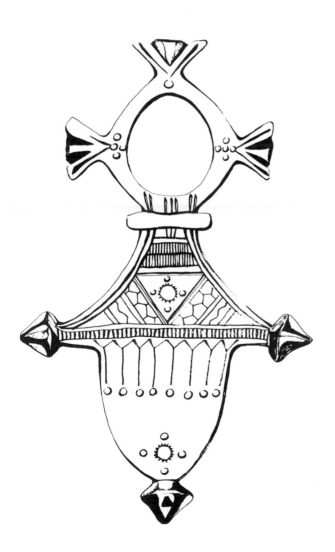

I. Approach

Although the two of us went to the Sahara first of all quite independently of one another – respectively, to look for remote prehistoric paintings on the Tassili N'Ajjer of southern Algeria, and to make a study of the history of the villages in southern Morocco – we met for the first time in Tamanrasset, an oasis in the foothills of the Hoggar Massif, Algeria, which was the starting point for an expedition on which we were both to work for the next few months. Within that year we were married and ever since then have returned to the Sahara together. Over the years, our interest in the Tuareg has developed steadily as our contact with them has become increasingly familiar and rewarding.

The Tuareg people are now broadly speaking nomads of the mountain ranges of the Aïr, the Hoggar and the Tassili N'Ajjer, surrounded by empty tracts of desert which do not afford easy access to European travellers. To reach these areas we have first to pass through the outlying wastes of North Africa, and whichever route we take we will encounter numerous other peoples, of contrasting cultures and ways of life. Among them we shall find the Mozabites, the Chaamba, the Tebu, the Hausa, the Peulh and the Arabs, with most of whom the Tuareg have at last learnt to co-exist quite comfortably, after generations of hostility and mistrust.

The route we have chosen for the purposes of this account is that which will be the route of days to come, as the smooth tarmac of the Trans-Saharan Highway forges its way through the barren landscapes of Algeria, Niger and southwards.

We start in the most northerly part of Africa, the Algerian coastline, which is not particularly different from certain parts of Europe in terms of terrain, climate, urban and agricultural development and so on. It is not until we have crossed the

Atlas Saharien, with its pyramids of snow, forests of pine and treacherous passes, that the great, windswept plains of Africa begin to stretch flatly before us. As night approaches, the towns dwindle to villages, the villages to nomadic encampments, and these to the stark empty desert, until there is nothing but the minute spark of a camp-fire around which a Berber family may be crouched – there to mind the goats and camels searching pasture.

Laghouat can be said to mark the beginning of the Sahara, but this is a Sahara of broken stones and bleak aridity, scored with channels carved by the melting snows of the Atlas mountains, gushing down to be absorbed by the desert; channels now dry, strewn only with thorny vegetation and, now and again, small birds like the black wheatear, hunting desperately for food. Originally known as El Aghouat, this sprawling town was once the Terminus of caravan routes from the south, and there-fore became a busy market centre for trading goods and negro slaves. Its recent development is directly related to the discovery of oil in the area, and although it is only one of the many oil towns of Algeria, it nevertheless contributes significantly to the all-important national economy.

Over a hundred miles south of Laghouat lies one of the few communities of northern Algeria to flourish without being in any way dependent on oil: Ghardaïa. As we penetrate more deeply into the desert, this is the next major settlement that we reach; it is astonishingly situated, hidden from view in the meandering valley of the M'zab, and breathtakingly picturesque. Its name means literally the Grotto of Daïa. As legend has it, Daïa was an old woman who fell back from her nomadic group as they moved on to new pastures, and was discovered, in a fire-lit grotto, by a sheikh who determined to take her as another of his wives and found a com-munity in her honour. To this day there is a shrine in the heart of Ghardaïa to her memory. The name is now used collectively to describe five towns: El-Atteuf, Ghardaïa, Beni-Isguen, Bou-Noura and Melika. Dotted along the valley within six miles of each other, each town has been constructed on the slopes of a prominent hill in the valley for defensive purposes. Originally, two further towns – Guerara and Berriane – were included within the settlement, but these broke away following political disagreements and are now re-established sixty and thirty miles from Ghardaïa respectively.

The first town was founded early in the eleventh century by a group of radically orthodox Moslems called Ibadites, originating from the Middle East, who had already made attempts to found their own community in this area at Tiaret and Ouargla. They had been consistently persecuted for their strict conservatism and were ultimately driven to the inhospitable desert, the heart of the *chebka*, which means literally 'network of stones', where they took refuge from the outside world.

Having fled this far they were at last able to live in peace, but they faced the new problem of how to exist in such a hostile landscape. The way this problem was solved is now a classic example of desert reclamation. The site chosen had only one advan-tage – the wide river bed of the M'zab, which was dry except on the rare occasions when rain fell, and even then the flow was brief. The Ibadites (who became known as Mozabites being the people of the M'zab) not only built a complicated irrigation system to utilize every pint of water that flowed, but also dug – by hand – deep wells along the valley from which to draw water. These exist today more or less as they did all those centuries ago. Extensive groves of orange trees, date palms and vegetables have been cultivated outside the walled towns, and to this day enough is produced to warrant the men travelling all the way up to Algiers to sell their goods, though nowadays they travel by lorry – and not by camel or horse. The women kept goats for milk, cheese and meat, and wove intricate carpets and prayer mats from the goats' hair, using natural vegetable dyes for colouring. Each house still has a loom of some scale in the kitchen, and the carpets, although less beautiful since the introduction of garish modern colours, are still famed throughout North Africa, and celebrated annually with the *Fête de Tapis du M'zab*.

The great fight for survival against the desert and the elements, as well as against wandering bands of brigands, made the Mozabites unusually industrious, and therefore correspondingly productive. Part of the fruit and vegetable markets in Algiers and one or two other big towns in the north came to belong solely to the Mozabites who, through their material success, were able to expand the palm groves and gardens of the M'zab valley. Not long after the founding of Ghardaïa, it had become a significant point on one of the great caravan trading routes between the north and the Sudan area, and it is still an important centre for trade in the northern Sahara. It had developed so successfully that even during the Algerian War of Independence in 1962 it was able to sustain a degree of uninvolvement, to continue farming as in peace time for the sake of its produce.

Through the centuries, because of a still rigorously upheld law that forbids anyone from one M'zab town to marry into another, there has been consistent intermarriage, a high infant mortality rate and a high proportion of physical abnormalities – particularly in eye-sight deficiency. Walking through the narrow and crowded cobbled alley-ways of any of the M'zab towns, we were immediately struck by the number of men with thick-lensed spectacles, supported by walking sticks or being led by a child. There were hardly any women to be seen, and those that were, were almost totally veiled, a custom stemming back from the earliest days of the Ibadite community. In those times, the men were already spending long periods away from home selling produce, and so they enforced a strict code of behaviour for the women. 'Factions' were formed, comprising several families, and an Elder was elected by the husbands as Faction Head, to stay at home to direct the material needs of the families while also acting as chaperon to every wife in his faction. To help him fulfil this role, certain 'deterrents' were instigated: no wife should even look at any man but her husband, she should never venture out of doors without being fully veiled and wrapped in a woven wool blanket obscuring everything but one eye, never be seen unveiled by a stranger even in her own house, never go outside without a female companion, and then only after sundown to avoid the public gaze. The *Muezzin* who calls the faithful to prayer five times a day from the top of the minaret, which is both the spiritual and architectural focal point of each town, has always been a blind man and thus unable to catch sight of the unveiled women on their terrace roof tops; even in the Mosque there is a separate chamber in which the women worship to avoid the risk of being confronted by any men, though in practice few women go to the Mosque as it is considered unsuitable to leave behind all the work that is (theoretically) piling up at home.

Despite all these efforts to encourage fidelity, wives whose husbands were absent for two or three years often continued to bear children regardless.

With the nearby presence of the oil rigs, affluent Europeans in the north, and increasing cynicism amongst the young Mozabites, the flavour of Ghardaïa is changing. Within the walls of the towns themselves, however, where no stranger is allowed to set foot after sundown, only slight changes have taken place during the last few hundred years; noticeable in this respect are the mosques built for the more progressive Mozabites, who prefer showers, taps with running water, and electric neon lighting in the ablutions chamber, to pouring the water out of the earthenware vessels of yesterday, by the dim light of oil lamps. Needless to say, the new mosques are much frowned on by the Elders.

Each town has a central market place surrounded by shady arcades where the elderly men meet every afternoon and where once or twice a week a market is held. Some have auctions which involve a lively and amusing ceremony. The town of Ghardaïa itself has a large market place, and holds a daily market, while every Friday all the other markets assemble here, so that the cobbled square is jammed with men in *djellabas* and close-fitting caps (which gives them a peculiarly Jewish appearance), bartering and trading anything from camels to kindling – which is brought in by the bundle on the backs of the nomads from the outlying desert and sold for next to nothing. The camels, goats and other live-stock are tethered but by no means passive, superimposing their roaring and scuffling above the clamour of men. Donkeys flanked with heavily laden saddle baskets jockey for position, tottering and sometimes falling, whereupon they have to be unloaded to get back onto their feet, while the spilt dates and oranges are surreptitiously seized by small hands.

On one of our first visits to this market, we were in the last stages of a day-long negotiation with a carpet vendor in a shadowy corner of the arcade, when the air was suddenly rent with gunfire – a series of abrupt rifle shots that silenced every other sound. We were very alarmed, until we saw the amused pleasure in the faces of all the local people, who were on tiptoe watching some spectacle in the midst of a solid ring of men. In the hush that followed the shattering explosions, we heard drums and hand-cymbals, though we couldn't actually see any dancing. The celebration was in honour of the newly elected Mayor, and the firing of blank cartridges was the crescendo of the traditional Chaamba folk dance; this we learnt from a grinning gremlin-like character who had been haggling for a second-hand soup ladle at the next stall when the shots had interrupted his flow. He was to tell us many things in his Arabic-cum-French, including the fact that he owned a restaurant and we looked in need of one of his meals. Since then we have had dozens of half-coherent exchanges with 'Moussa', in the noisy, sawdust-on-the-floor 'Café de la Paix' where cats sleep on top of the vast wooden refrigerator, children lurk in the shadows and Moussa shouts at the world with gaiety and abandon from behind an ominous screen of blackened steaming cauldrons. About the festivities in the market that day, he smiled indulgently, and began to explain in his curious language the reason why he couldn't take it seriously: to see the once hated, dreaded Chaamba tribesmen actually being hired to entertain Mozabites in the middle of Ghardaïa – when at one time the Mozabites would not even have acknowledged their presence – was to him incomprehensible. Moussa is a Chaamba himself, from the Chaamba centre of Metlili, about fifteen miles south of Ghardaïa. For centuries, the Chaamba were the Mozabites' greatest enemies. An Arab tribe, renowned throughout this part of the world for their ruthlessness, greed and aggresion, they settled in Metlili in the fourteenth century – probably with the express intention of profiting from the wealth of the now flourishing M'zab valley. Metlili has the same advantages as the walled towns of the M'zab: built on a promontory, it commands a wide view of the surrounding desert, yet is not easily visible from just one mile away, and thus formed a perfect stronghold for a people such as the Chaamba. It became a refuge for all sorts of bandits and outlaws from the area, some of whom inevitably joined forces with the Chaamba, whose power consequently became greater and more feared than any other in the land. In fact, Ghardaïa was to suffer at the hands of the Chaamba right up to the period of French colonial rule from 1848 to 1961, when the raiding and plundering that had always gone on in the desert was to a great extent suppressed, making way for a state of relatively amicable co-existence.

Some aspects of the Chaamba way of life compare with that of the Tuareg, although ethnically the two tribes are unrelated. Their nomadism, their camel rearing and their raiding and terrorizing exploits are the obvious common denominators, and it could be said that the Chaamba were to the northern Sahara what the Tuareg were to the south: the All-Powerful, to whom high tolls or bribes were paid in return for guaranteed safety while travelling in the desert. This did not, however, draw them towards each other as allies; on the contrary, the Chaamba were responsible for the final and irrefutable defeat of the Hoggar Tuareg – whom we meet in Tamanrasset – at the famous Battle of Tit, only a few miles north of Tamanrasset, in 1902, under the auspices of the French Camel Corps and Lieutenant Cottonest. The Chaamba were practised in warfare and made willing mercenaries, but the Tuareg of the Hoggar were ill-equipped to meet the challenge of modern firearms, and lost ninety-three men of a total company of less than three hundred, as opposed to a loss of four men on the Chaamba side. The Hoggar Tuareg were overpowered morally as much as physically, forced to accept that their supremacy was finished; they were never to engage in any full-scale battles again.

Although Moussa did not tell us all the above, he gave us a not very articulate but sufficiently interesting account to arouse our curiosity. As we met more Chaamba, in other scattered oases, we felt indebted to him as we were then able more or less to complete the picture.

Moussa's menu is an odd assortment of Algerian *cous-cous* (tiny balls of rolled and steamed semolina with a spicy vegetable sauce, and sometimes meat), *chorba*, which is a clear vegetable and noodle soup with a distinctive parsley-like herb, thick chick-pea stew, spaghetti, cold chips, fried camel liver, camel steak (described as *bif-tek*) or macaroni soup, with a constant flow of dates, oranges, little glasses of mint tea and animated chatter; we have never found a Saharan café as lively.

Moussa's home, on the other side of the narrow street and up a dark staircase, rank with the smell of rotting meat, has a much more extrovert quality than any Mozabite's: it is a happy, shambling cacophony of children, kittens, hares, pregnant wives, hens and goats, co-existing rowdily in a smoke-filled atmosphere that causes constant coughing. It proved a strong contrast to our first visit to a typically Mozabite home in Beni-Isguen, the most orthodox of all the Ghardaïan towns whose name means literally the Holy City. We were ushered down a deserted street and into a short low-vaulted tunnel, through an elaborately locked door, and quickly into a small room. Our host watched us take off our shoes, then left us. Silent as a church, the room had a consecrated air about it, with icon-like wall hangings, thick sound-swallowing carpets and cushions to sit on, opulent-looking brass trays and tables with Arabic inscriptions, prayers from the Koran. Our host bustled back in with a jug of soured milk, and a basket filled with top quality dates. After half an hour's almost whispered conversation, a small girl, consumed by shyness, crept in with a tea-tray: silver tea-pot, kettle, glasses, sugar and tea, her face half-hidden by her luminous green nylon headscarf. While her father prepared the tea she forced herself (or her mother forced her) to tiptoe quickly back in with an ornamental tray of almond biscuits, blushing and hiding behind her arm in confusion. Our host was accustomed to outsiders as he was often cast in the role of City Guide because of his good French and fluent manner, guides being compulsory for any visitor to Beni-Isguen. His flow of information proved at times to contradict itself but was delivered with great conviction. On certain grounds he was very firm: there was no smoking in Beni-Isguen (a scandal had almost been caused on the way to his house as one of our companions had taken cigarettes from his pocket), and the honesty amongst the townspeople was unequalled anywhere. This had to be demonstrated by our leaving several hundred pounds' worth of photographic equipment on the pavement of a crowded market for two hours. He had made his point, but he reinforced the statement by further claims to the morality of the people: thieves, drunkards and liars did not exist; it was a city without vice, with no place for prisons or even policemen . . .

The City Wall is a double one, because the original, inner wall could not contain the growing population. The townspeople couldn't move elsewhere, being forbidden to marry into another town, so the town had to expand. New boundaries were constructed, and a crude adobe look-out tower of considerable height stands on the perimeter, overlooking a long stretch of the valley as well as the whole of the town. It is said to have been built by all the men of Beni-Isguen within a single day.

In the no-man's-land outside the walled towns, where the young congregate, there are many signs of progress and development: modern post office, bank, hospital, motor-scooter shops, brand new cinema and a football ground for the local youth –

not to mention the updated hotels, with central heating in winter, swimming pools, French cuisine, and bars decked with every kind of bottle, the latter forming the nucleus of such night life as there is at Ghardaïa. The scruffier the hotel, the cheaper the anisette and the drunker the clientele; brawls and fights are the invariable outcome of a 'sociable' evening, which is a very far cry from the devout and reverend quiet that descends on the ancient walled towns after sunset. The oil rigs within the vicinity of Ghardaïa, staffed mainly by Europeans and Americans, sometimes put an embargo on all alcohol in the camp, so that on their rare visits to town the men are thirsty for drink and diversion, and anxious to get rid of some of the local currency which forms a part of their salaries. This is a contributing factor to the atmosphere of the bars.

All in all, on leaving Ghardaïa and clambering back out of the M'zab valley onto the gravel plains of the desert, the impressions we take away with us are varied: the complex of towns and palmgroves, busy streets and silent mosques, are full of contrast and contradiction, as are the people themselves – some clinging desperately to their hard-won heritage, others adopting the 'easy life' of the twentieth century with all its impermanency. Perhaps these are the very reasons why so many tourists now flock here from northern Algeria and Europe, on holiday and for fêtes. In the past they were not made welcome, nor were any facilities provided for them, but now Ghardaïa is beginning to capitalize upon the interest she can attract from abroad.

Once back upon the road, bowling across the unmitigating tedium of the *reg* or rock desert, whose horizons disappear in a shimmer of heat, it is as though the Ghardaïa episode was entirely imaginary: the lush and thriving oasis seems to be swallowed at one gulp, and is now in fact visible only from the air – from where, like a lop-sided starfish, it can be seen extending its limbs along the *wadi* tributaries, always culminating in a mass of palm-greenery and whitewashed houses huddling around the mosque and minaret.

The pace is regular and predictable on the route southwards, the rise and fall of the wind being the only changeable element. At times the tarmac is buried under tons of wind-blown sand, which is shifted periodically by a sand plough. Wherever the road is most prone to this condition there are signs saying 'Sand' in Arabic and French, as there are also signs illustrating a camel where herds are grazing on the negligible pastures. These, then, are the only interruptions we are likely to meet, apart from one or two other vehicles: either heavy lorries from the road construction site at the end of the road on which we are travelling, or the Taxi – a Citroën saloon – that does a daily double-run from Ghardaïa to the next oasis south, El-Goléa, about one hundred and fifty miles each way, packed solid with passengers. The road now and again contains a wide curve, now and again is carved through a rocky outcrop, occasionally runs across the floor of a meandering *wadi* or river bed. But at one stage, on rounding a gravelly hillock, a lone building appears on the right hand side: even more unexpectedly, there is a crudely written sign on the roadside, reading Café-Restaurant, with an arrow. We have never failed to stop here, although at times in vain. A massive metal gate in a high wall opens onto a sand-swept deserted courtyard, in the middle of which are the relics of a deep well, surrounded by the cleanly stripped and bleached branches of erstwhile exotic foliage and banked on each side by piles of sand through which poke empty Coca-Cola bottles. There are darkened rooms off the courtyard, in one of which we expect to find our Arab friend. Invariably he has to be wakened from a deep sleep in a corner somewhere, his head covered by his *djellaba* against the indefatigable flies. He produces glasses of thick brown coffee, sweetened with condensed milk on a half-and-half basis which he insists is the only civilized way to serve coffee: '. . . after the French recipe' he repeats doggedly. This establishment was built by the French, and was once a flourishing base camp for the French Army, the courtyard a well-kept garden with abundant fruit trees and flowers, surrounded by kitchens, rest-rooms and store-rooms. The Arab remembers it as if it were yesterday. Now the wind whistles through the rooms, the sand floats over the walls into the coffee, and the sun glares down. The Sahara is punctuated everywhere with just such examples of how the desert will reclaim any land which man does not struggle very hard to keep fertile.

Reinvigorated, we proceed south and in the distance we begin to see not the glinting and sun-reflecting hardness of stones, but dense masses of sand-dunes. Like the sand-ripples of the sea-shore enormously enlarged, these dunes run towards the road, are heaped up beside the road, and in places reach half-way across the road. Wherever there is even a gentle incline we are allowed a brief glimpse of the expansive sand sea of the Grand Erg Occidental – red brown dunes undulating into infinity.

The road zig-zags down through a steep precipice, and out onto a flat sandy plain in the midst of which a highly active community exists beneath the generous shade of large and leafy trees. A sprawling blot of dark green on the warm earth tones of the desert, El-Goléa seems compact from the exposed road above, but its population is spread – if thinly – over an extensive area. The outskirts have recently sprouted rows of stark, grey breeze-block houses, crudely finished, the front yards separated with panels of corrugated iron, creating an atmosphere of dereliction, of failed suburbia, unsoftened by any humanizing element in the hostile desert landscape. Women and girls, in their diaphanous, day-glo dresses, are shy of strangers and always keep in the background, but the men are overtly friendly and cheerful.

One of the few things that the people of the Sahara have in plenty and to spare, is time; hours may be passed in convivial exchanges in the street, as everyone walks, rides a donkey or cycles about his daily task, and there is never any excuse to hurry. Anyone with a tight schedule or an impatient disposition soon learns about frustration in an oasis like this one. Queueing for a stamp in the post office – an imposing new building on the main square – can take half a day, as everyone in turn diverts the clerk with apparently inconsequential chatter; when your own turn comes, the chances are that he will have sold out of stamps, until the arrival of the next plane!

In any remote oasis, the weekly flights are known to nearly everyone, as the planes play such an important part in supplying the town, particularly with perishable goods, and in communications. The activities of the airport, a landing strip and an informal group of buildings on the edge of the town, provide something of a focal point for the local youth, who congregate to watch the arrivals and departures with interest. In the same way, the hospital waiting room provides the women of the oasis with an unofficial meeting place, as they are deprived of any recognized social centre. This we learnt from a young Frenchman undergoing his military service as a dentist in El-Goléa. All his patients had a chronic disrespect for their teeth, but enjoyed nothing more than having rows of gold fillings in their mouths, which they consistently dislodged by cracking hard nuts or dried dates with them. He told us that the waiting room was always packed with chattering women, none of whom were ailing save from the boredom of being isolated in their own homes all their lives.

The other meeting place for the women is the Turkish Baths, which are quite an experience. The darkened rooms, lit by an orange glow and filled with billowing steam, are loud with a high-pitched female clamour, and the murky water is ankle deep. On first entering, the thick perfume-laden air is suffocating and all-obscuring, but gradually a primitive scene is revealed of naked female forms in all shapes and sizes and different attitudes, chatting and laughing together, uninhibited for once, closeted in an excessively hot and vapour-filled room.

In the palm grove outside El-Goléa is a small catholic church called St. Joseph's, near to a ruined fort now partially submerged in rolling dunes, in a scene of tranquility and solitude. Beside the church is the tomb of the well-known catholic missionary, the Père de Foucauld, who died in Tamanrasset in 1916, but whose story becomes more relevant further south.

Our first port of call on arrival in El-Goléa is usually the *Syndicat d'Initiative*, whose staff are particularly friendly and informal. This is a Shop-cum-Information Centre, run by the town and common to every Saharan oasis. As well as locally collected prehistoric arrowheads, axeheads, beads carved from ostrich eggshell and desert roses, this one has especially fine weaving, embroidery and carpets for sale, which are produced by the White Sisters, an order of nuns who have a centre in El-Goléa and do a lot of the hospital work.

The prehistoric artefacts at the *Syndicat d'Initiative* are most impressive for their sheer quantity, perhaps more than for their quality, and this is also true of the desert roses. These are a form of crystallized gypsum that remotely resemble the formation of a flower, and are dug up in the sandy desert. During one of our longer visits to El-Goléa we were entertained and intrigued to be invited to participate in a desert rose hunt, by our friends at the *Syndicat*. This entailed an early start on a bright morning, with much panic as to whether we had enough food to last the day, not to mention tea, and an hour's drive along the open road, before hitting the rough desert terrain as we branched off at right angles. We drove our own Landrover, and our three hosts guided us over rocky hills and deep sandy *wadis*, until we reached an open plain upon which, on closer scrutiny, we could see these extraordinary mineral formations 'growing'. Above ground they were very brittle, but on digging down several feet – an energetic exercise under the Saharan sun – it was possible to raise some large, very heavy and perfectly intact examples. Triumphantly we excavated until we felt too weak to dig another spade of sand, though even so we had hardly made a mark on the whole plain, which was covered with these 'roses' as far as the eye could see. The late lunch produced by our friends, of soup, roast rabbit and bread, was gratifying, and fortifying in view of the hazardous drive back: laden with weighty desert roses the return route was still less navigable and time after time we were stuck in the soft sand, pushing and heaving until nightfall – our friends flatly refusing to jettison any of their hard-won booty. At long last we reached the oasis, where a nightcap of mint-tea was more than welcome. But the day was not complete until we had met the pet creature that lives in a box in a drawer: a three-inch transparent yellow scorpion, which managed to escape from its box and run frantically around the room with its tail arched viciously over its head. We shuddered with discomfort until it was recaptured, whereupon, of course, we were told that it was without sting. This seems to typify the odd sense of humour demonstrated by the desert dweller!

During the sixteenth century, a splinter group of Chaamba from Metlili, known as the Mouadhi Chaamba, moved south to El-Goléa because of the growing internal unrest amongst the Chaamba in the north. Here they settled, building an ambitious fort – now ruined – around the summit of a towering hill which overshadows the oasis. This fort was utilized by the French during the last century, but its original purpose was as a defence against the Tuareg, in case they should dare to venture so far north. The present-day population of El-Goléa is largely made up of Arabs from Chaamba descent.

Like Ghardaïa, El-Goléa has its mosques and minarets, but here the *Muezzin* at the top of the minaret is replaced by a recorded disc that is played five times a day to summon the devoted to prayer, the needle sometimes getting stuck so that sections of the disc become very familiar! The amplification of the disc is something of an electrical feat: its monotonous chanting can be heard loud and clear in every house for many streets, awaking and rousing not only the devoted (to which anyone who has stayed in either of the two hotels will doubtless bear witness).

A new hotel, 'high-rise like a real Hilton' we were informed, is to become a feature of the skyline of El-Goléa in the very near future. This obviously represents a great threat to an oasis the size of El-Goléa, in that the slow, strolling pace of life will come to an end. With the glamour of a Luxury Desert Hotel, tourists will pour in by road and plane, restaurants, cinemas, shops and banks will mushroom, the quality of the craftsmanship will deteriorate to meet the increased demand, folk-lore such as the Chaamba dancing and camel riding will become commercialized, and a newness will mask all that is ancient and traditional in the oasis.

Allied to this, the swift, smooth tarmac road, on which we drove down to El-Goléa, is continuing steadily southwards – destined to reach Tamanrasset within the next few years. Superficially, this is no more than yet another symptom of the changing world, as is the installation of electricity in the oasis, and the advent of the telephone. But with this road, the Trans-Saharan Highway, the gates are opened to the desert. No longer will the planning and forethought of expedition-travel be needed to cross

El-Goléa: part of the oasis viewed from the ruins of the Chaamba fort

A typical Targui of the Hoggar with his Tuareg camel saddle. Peak Laperrine may be seen in the background

the Sahara: cars and buses will be quite equal to the task and tourism will invade even the smallest and quietest villages along the route almost overnight.

As always, there are many sides to this vexed question of making remote and relatively untouched areas accessible to the whole world. Economically the country will benefit, as will the local business people, and there is a degree of inevitability about 'progress'. It will also mean a sure death to many other aspects of life in the Saharan environment.

Separating El-Goléa from the Hoggar Massif and the oases of the south, is a rugged plateau – the Tademaït – which has always acted as a natural barrier between the Chaamba- and Tuareg-dominated lands. Just north of it is a long-abandoned French Foreign Legion Fort, Fort Mirabelle. Built around the turn of the century, it was overthrown within the space of a year by Chaamba nomads, since when it has only been re-inhabited briefly. It is now a camping ground for any passing traffic, so that gleaming empty cans, broken glass, cardboard and paper litter are the sole furnishings, and vipers the sole residents, of this desolate and sordid fort.

Crossing the Tademaït Plateau is hazardous even today; during the winter months, a little rain transforms the powdery red sand into a quagmire of treacherous and sinking mud – a serious threat to vehicles – so that it is often necessary to make a detour via Timimoun and Adrar, which adds hundreds of miles to the route. In summer the mud, and the ruts caused by heavy lorries, are petrified into granite hardness, with a coating of dust which is churned up by every moving vehicle, insinuating itself into and onto everything in sight. The Tademaït is an uninhabited plateau and lacking in any redeeming features, with rough ground, no significant landmarks, and no vegetation or wildlife. It is always with a great sigh of relief that we spot the narrow white ribbon of track as it winds down off the plateau onto the plain that leads us towards In Salah, a plain dotted with conical mountains and outcrops of slate grey rock.

When we first arrived at El-Goléa we were impressed by the sensation of being in a true oasis, but In Salah – which means the Well of Allah – is a much more striking and severe example, the most forbidding in the entire Sahara. Strong winds blow, lifting the sands, shifting the dunes. The whole town is half-submerged in a relentless encroachment of the outlying desert, and with the exception of the few calm days, the inhabitants spend as little time as possible out of doors. The walled market has scant produce, and we have never seen it alive with bartering, yelling customers like the other Saharan markets; the hotel, whose windows are broken and whose doors clatter in the wind, no longer functions; and the only figures to be seen are swathed in cloaks, heads bent against the stinging sand in the wind.

In Salah, or Tuat as the region is still known to the older generation, has been a significant oasis on the itinerary of trading caravans from the south for centuries. Although it never developed into a major market, it used to be a changing post for caravans, where camels and men were replaced for the final leg of the journey, the tired ones resting up for the long march back. Thus goods did indeed change hands, and business was transacted on a large scale, but only amongst a transitory population: people who came in one day and left the next. It never grew to the proportions of some cities of the desert, despite its importance as a watering and cargo-transferring centre. One of the last caravan trails to survive in this part of the Sahara – in spite of the heavy competition from lorries – is the In Salah to Ouargla route, which passes through forgotten desert wastes where few people exist.

The explorer, Gordon Laing – who was the first non-African to reach Timbuctou voluntarily – spent five weeks at In Salah on his way down in 1825, where he was the object of great fascination, being the only white man to have stayed in the oasis at that time. Laing dismissed the place as unworthy of much comment, claiming that there was little to interest anyone there. Not long after he left, his caravan was attacked at night by a band of raiding Tuareg, who wounded him very badly and stole all his vital possessions, but it was a *Targui,* or Tuareg man, who had befriended him during his period at In Salah.

These days the population of In Salah is sedentary, and a living is scratched out of the desert, where the palm groves are buffeted by the constant wind, and the gardens are always under attack from the sand. Motorized traffic calls there for fuel and water, much as the camel caravans had to in the past, but nowadays, far from taking several days, the task can be accomplished within an hour, including checking in at the town hall, and buying bottles of ice-cold drinks.

Although In Salah is predominantly Arab, it is here that we first catch a glimpse of any Tuareg, conspicuous in their elaborate turban-like head-dress (*taguelmoust*) and flowing cotton robes, but most distinctive for their slenderness and their height when compared to their neighbours. The initial impact of the Tuareg, however, is very much greater in Tamanrasset, so we will not dwell on them here, but proceed southwards to the Hoggar mountains and Tamanrasset.

After the tedious journey over the Tademaït, the stage due south of In Salah seems almost picturesque, with a varying landscape of sands untrodden, interspersed with islands of massive black rocks, and a long meandering gorge through which the well-worn track snakes from side to side, dotted with flowering shrubs.

Since the first time we travelled this stretch of desert, the track has been regularly levelled with various crude implements, the most usual consisting of several tractor or lorry tyres chained together on their sides and dragged behind a vehicle, their sheer weight raking up the loose surface and distributing it more evenly.

Our first experience of this terrain was from the back of a thirty-ton articulated lorry that was deficient in brakes and suspension. Apart from the incessant jolting and banging – if we let go for a moment we were thrown at once to the opposite side of the truck – the dust was insufferable, clouds of it swirling around us in a thick fog all day, so that we were unable to gain any impression of the scenery through which we were passing. Luckily, our driver – an alcoholic from Algiers – had a deeply religious assistant who had to stop and pray five times a day. Had it not been for him we would probably never have stopped and would have been shaken to pieces. The driver had a specially protected bottle hanging from his door handle from which he gulped neat liquor all day, growing ever merrier and more reckless, until – towards sundown – he collapsed across the seats in the cab and slept for several hours. At this point the rest of us were able to uncover our faces, breathe the clean air and start to cook an evening meal. With the twilight, the wind would invariably drop and the desert would take on a different dimension, silent, cool and peaceful. Stars and moon shone with brilliance every night, silhouetting the lorry, now still, passive and inanimate, on the skyline. When the driver awoke, he washed and shaved and joined us all for the meal, incorrigibly cheerful and gay. Considering the size of his vehicle and the state of the track, we were most impressed that he hadn't had any trouble in the soft sand, or in negotiating the corridors of rock we encountered in places – but it transpired that he had been driving that stretch of desert for twenty-five years. He always woke first in the morning, starting up the motor of the lorry to wake the rest of us while the stars were still paling and the dawn was breaking over the night sky, to begin another day's rattling and bumping and dust. That journey lasted eight days, while now we can do it easily in three, so quickly are the distances in the desert diminishing.

We are nearing the Hoggar region at last, and beside the track we now see small Tuareg settlements of one or two families only, in dilapidated huts made from palm branches, with enclosed yards and a feeble fence acting as a windbreak. At one settlement we have a long-standing friendship with the family, originally established when we were able to help an ailing baby by giving the mother a supply of dried milk and sugar. In recent years, times have been very hard for the nomadic people in the Sahara as the rainfall has dropped to almost nothing. The drought is causing hundreds of animals to die every year, and the people exist on the threshold of starvation. Whenever we see this particular Tuareg family, we are unfailingly humbled by their courage and optimism. The women greet us with smiles and warmth, the youngest children hiding shyly amongst their skirts. When the men arrive, we are always invited to have green tea with them, and this is a time for joking and laughing, and remembering happy times, however worried and anxious they may be feeling about the future. Traditionally the Tuareg are brought up not to demonstrate negative emotions, whether grief, pain, distress or suspicion. Even their anger, which can blaze in their eyes, does not find expression in words. They are taught that it is undignified to seem anything other than serenely contented and carefree, however miserable their lot in life.

After some time spent in the company of this family, we begin to recognize in ourselves a sense of excitement and anticipation: we have arrived once more in the land of the Tuareg.

As a backdrop to the road-side settlements, mountain ranges supersede each other into infinity through fading shades of grey: we are approaching the foothills of the Hoggar Massif, and nearing the village of Tit, mentioned earlier for its historic battle. This is a Tuareg village, consisting of adobe houses and low nomad tents that resemble the wings of a gigantic outstretched bat hovering over the desert surface. Nowadays, the men and children of this village have learnt that to race frantically towards any passing traffic may well be rewarded by presents of chewing-gum, cigarettes, sweets, aspirins, or whatever the unthinking tourist may have to spare, and that they may even be able to sell their personal belongings for extortionate prices as 'souvenirs'. Their personal belongings have thus come to lack quality now, since they are produced as fast as possible to sell, with no care invested in them. Only a few years ago, the inherent Tuareg dignity would never have permitted this behaviour: the combination of their own desperate circumstances, and the opening offered to the opportunist when confronted by a hoard of wealthy tourists, has started to break down their pride.

Tamanrasset announces itself unmistakably by the transition to paved road: the sudden hush as the tyres roll off the clattering rubble and onto smooth tarmac. The airport building comes into view; pylons and telegraph poles begin to flash by, and then at last the dense mass of dusty tamarisk trees lies directly ahead.

II. The Hoggar Mountains

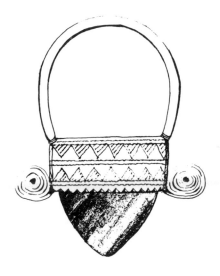

II. The Hoggar Mountains

It is impossible to say how many Tuareg there are today, or even how far afield they are scattered. In general terms a Saharan people, neither Arab, Berber nor Negro, they have been in the Sahara for at least a thousand years but have very gradually been pushed further south, firstly as result of pressure from the Arab invasion of North Africa, which began to affect them as long ago as the eighth century, and then more recently by the arrival of the European powers on the scene. For centuries they have successfully resisted domination, but there are now signs amongst the more northerly Tuareg tribes of their succumbing to Arab rule. In Tamanrasset, for example, it is a common sight to see a long, despondent queue of Tuareg outside the Algerian equivalent of the Labour Exchange, waiting to be given work. Traditionally, this is unheard of, and the very word for 'work' does not exist in the Tuareg language! But attempts are being made in many directions to 'urbanize' these primitive people, on the pretext of For Their Own Good.

They were converted from Paganism to Islam by the Arabs, but the Islam they have adopted has, to a certain extent, had their own interpretation stamped upon it. The Koran plays a vital part in their lives and even in their mythology, but they have maintained their own laws and customs relating to the government of their people, the structure of their society, the status of their women, and so on. There are some, inevitably, who are more devout than others, and there is the dichotomy of having accepted the religion of the Arabs without accepting the Arabs themselves. Even today, Arabic is a foreign language to them, and applied only as an extension of the Faith. We have met many Tuareg who regard the Arabs as their enemies, going so far as to join forces with Christian Europeans against the Arabs in wars as recent as that of Algerian Independence in 1962. *Tamarshak* is still the language in which they speak among themselves, sing, recite poems and tell stories. It is a powerful-sounding language, apparently rich in imagery, with certain similarities to the Berber dialects, but it is an over-simplification to relate the origins of the Tuareg too closely with those of the Berbers. The *tamarshak* vocabulary is bound by the comparative limitations of the Tuareg experience; as new experiences occur, existing foreign words are adopted to describe them (whether Arabic, French or Hausa, according to the language of the country they inhabit) which creates a curious linguistic mixture, but also helps to preserve the *tamarshak* language in its pure form without subjecting it to 'modernization'.

The written language, *tifinagh*, is even more restricted than the spoken in its breadth of expression, used chiefly as a means of communicating very straightforward ideas. Thus a nomadic group might leave a laboriously engraved message on the rocks, stating that 'the well up the *wadi* is dry'. The more creative and imaginative use of language remains in the spoken word and the memory.

A nomadic existence may impose a less rigid discipline regarding religious practices in that there is no formal mosque in which to worship, no *Muezzin* to adhere to and no minarets pointing heavenwards to serve as a daily reminder. But at the same time the dictates of a nomadic way of life are in some ways more conducive to following a strict code of behaviour than is an urban existence: there is no pork, and no alcohol; fasting – through necessity rather than choice – becomes second nature to the nomad, and the specified times of prayer incorporate well into the day's routine; so, some of the temptations removed, there are fewer sacrifices to be made. Although four wives are permitted, it is most unusual for the Targui to take more than one, partly due to practicalities such as the economics involved, and partly because every woman plays a significant part in the community. A certain amount of mystique has been allowed to develop on this subject, and many people now think of the Tuareg as a matriarchal, matrilineal society, which is not strictly accurate. The highly distinctive form of dress of the Tuareg men compared to that of their women has helped to foster this fallacy: during adolescence the men take on a veil head-dress, the *taguelmoust*, which consists of an elaborately arranged length of light cotton, sometimes as much as six metres in length, concealing the scalp and lower face entirely, without which in theory they are never to be seen for the rest of their days. Contrary to Moslem tradition elsewhere, the women are bare-faced and frequently bare-headed, but there is no reason to connect this apparent reversal of roles with the supremacy or superiority of the women. However, it is correct to say that whatever status is held by the mother is inherited by her offspring, rather than that of the father being inherited. Likewise, a man can 'better himself' socially by marrying a woman of higher rank than himself, while a woman retains the rank of her birth whomever she marries. It is also true that a woman can own property prior to marriage and still keep it after marriage, while her husband has to share whatever he has and be completely responsible for her and their children on his own initiative.

A Targui with the broad taguelmoust and heavy woven-wool over-garment worn in winter

Tuareg women and children outside a zeriba – a hut constructed from palm fronds – in the Hoggar Mountains

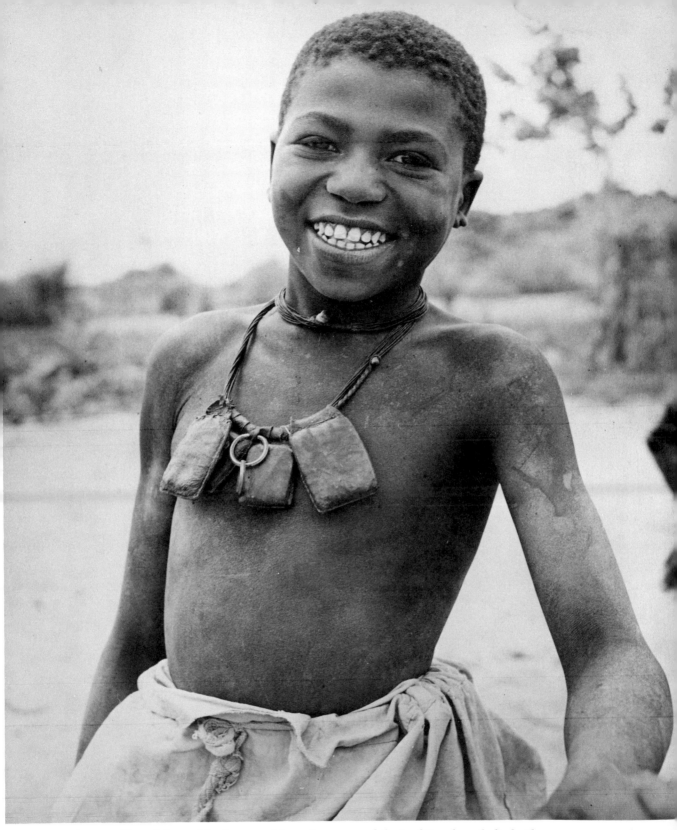

*A young Targui dressed in the ragged loose trousers and the traditional symbolic leather orna-
mentation of his people*

A Targuia with her baby. The child's head has been shaved but for the top and crown, by which he would be raised to heaven if he died in infancy

Tuareg children are named, however, in such a way as to retain their father's name, not – as is popularly supposed – their mother's. For instance, a common name like Mohamed Ben Sidi means literally Mohamed, son of Sidi. In the event of the father dying, it is the mother's elder brother who takes on the responsibility of the children, and, to complicate things further, a man's wealth is often inherited by the children of his eldest sister, the boys receiving twice as much as the girls, following the Moslem custom.

With regard to marriage, each partner is traditionally from the same clan, but not from the same camp, and not closely related, so that first cousins never marry. Women generally marry at the age of twenty to twenty-five, while the men are nearer to thirty years old. After marriage the couple lives for about a year in the same camp as the parents of the bride, and then moves over to join the husband's parents, unless, by some chance, they come from different clans, when they are likely to stay with the bride's family forever. Divorce is unusual, as is adultery, though neither is unheard of by any means. In the event of a man being unfaithful to his wife, she will generally simply pack up and return to her own people; if the man is wronged he is entitled to kill both his wife and her lover. This rarely happens, of course, and more often than not a man will forgive his wife under such circumstances, and take no action, but he can enforce a fine on the third party through the Amenokal if he wants to pursue it.

All the governing of Tuareg communities is conducted by men, except in the rare instances where a 'noble' woman is invited to offer her counsel on an especially difficult issue.

There is a Tuareg proverb which summarizes the relationship between the men and women very aptly: 'Man and women towards each other are for the eyes and for the heart, and not only for the bed' – which immediately sets them a long way apart from the Arabs.

The class and clan system of the Tuareg becomes very complicated, when studied in detail: the whole race is divided into confederations, which are sub-divided into tribes, which are again sub-divided into clans, which are finally divided into factions. Nowadays, however, all these divisions are less easily recognizable as the Tuareg become increasingly obsessed with the struggle to survive, tending to consolidate as one entity in order to escape being wiped off the face of the earth by drought, starvation and governmental pressure to conform. In terms of prestige, three main divisions used to apply: the nobles always occupied the highest rung of the ladder, followed by the vassals, and lastly by the 'slaves' together with various minority sections of the society. Slavery in the real sense has now been abolished. No longer do bands of Tuareg raiders steal out under the cloak of darkness to attack camel caravans on the move, to rob them of the Negroes brought up from the south, and subsequently incorporate them into the Tuareg community as slaves. No longer are there minutely planned ambushes in the desert plains for the same ends, and thus no longer are there any true slaves amongst the Tuareg. But the descendents of such slaves still live with the Tuareg, and are still regarded as somewhat inferior. Even when slavery was at its height, however, the slaves were well catered for and cared for as far as we can determine. This was pointed up by the fact that when offered the chance of complete freedom, the majority of the slaves refused it – or accepted it and eventually returned to their 'masters'. They were comfortable, without responsibilities, and with a guaranteed livelihood – with even the right to own and manage their own land and livestock in some of the sedentary communities – and they knew only too well that to be turned loose in the Sahara to try to make a living would spell almost certain disaster. On the other hand, it is just as difficult for too large a group of nomads to try to survive as one unit in these conditions: difficult because of the quickly exhausted pasture for the animals, and the insufficient supplies of water for all the thirsty mouths. For these reasons, the normal size of a group of nomads does not exceed two or three dozen people. If the pasture is good, it may support their livestock for a few months, but on occasion they settle for a matter of days only. They always have to settle within walking distance of a supply of water, which also presents obvious problems, for even if the pasture is plentiful, it is useless without access to water.

One section of the Tuareg society worthy of particular mention, although a relatively small one, is that occupied by the silver-smiths, or *Inadin*. Still shrouded by a certain amount of mystery, the smiths are a wandering nomadic Saharan group who move constantly from one established camp to the next; on arrival they are made welcome because of their usefulness, but they are, simultaneously, despised for their shabby and unkempt appearance and their almost vagrant way of life. Their practical ability is not restricted to silver smithing, although they are excellent craftsmen in this field; the *Inadin* also act as surgeons, woodcarvers and fortune-tellers whenever the need arises. Perhaps their paramount function, however, has developed through their readiness to carry messages from one group to another: they are frequently used as go-betweens, for clandestine lovers, or for heads of tribes, and in this way they virtually become the *confidants* of the parties involved. This relationship has only been made possible through the extreme diplomacy and discretion of the *Inadin*, as well as through their being forever on the move. Physically they retain all the characteristics of the rest of the Tuareg, but their dress is of much less formal presentation; the *taguelmoust* is usually in tatters and is wound sloppily around the head, and the rest of the clothes are likely to have been passed down from some well-disposed person from one of the camps at which the smith calls regularly.

The group leaders of the normal Tuareg communities, who might be nobles or high-ranking vassals, spend most of their lives on the move, scouting for sufficient pasture and water to warrant a camp; as soon as one camp is established, they set off to search for the next. These days, the chief motivation of the Tuareg nomads is survival: to win the struggle against the constant threat of drought. A hundred years ago there were feuds to be settled, wars and battles to be fought, and raids to be accomplished. There was much less time for domestic concerns, and the intrigue was intense, demanding great secrecy and subterfuge. They were not then faced with anything like the existing problem of lack of vegetation for the animals. Rainfall used to be higher, and goats – so destructive to plant life – were less prolific. Considering the very name of the Tassili N'Ajjer, literally the Plateau of the Goats, it is hardly surprising that the pasture is now paltry, all the shrubs and grasses having been wrenched up by their roots, instead of being bitten off to grow again.

We know of one family whose entire livestock was destroyed by the lack of rain in recent years. This so crippled the family economy that they were forced to move down from the mountains and settle near an administrative centre where there would be a chance of employment for the men. This is becoming a common story in some parts: reluctantly the Tuareg adopt a new way of life, taking the line of least resistance to authority, because the only alternative is gradual starvation. So the fabric of their lives disintegrates: there are schools that the children have to attend, there are houses that the families have to inhabit. The traditional dress is put away, to be replaced by the uniform of the road-builder or the lorry driver. No more are there long evenings around the camp fire telling stories, laughing and teasing with faces animated in the red glow of the firelight beneath the protective shadows of the rocks, and no more are there spontaneous folk festivals, or romantic *soirées* for the young. After sundown each family is isolated within its four walls – the four walls of respectability and progress. But even now there are Tuareg who are prepared to travel vast distances in search of more hospitable terrain, in order to escape the fate of their suppressed brothers: to be able to live as they have always lived, to move freely, to sleep beneath an empty sky at night, and tread the untrodden paths, whose vistas and horizons are forever changing.

Year by year, the numbers of Tuareg based on the town of Tamanrasset increase, and for many of them, the nomadic life has already drawn to a close. Encircled by the dense grey mountains and looming peaks of the Hoggar foothills, on the edge of a sprawling sandy *wadi*, Tamanrasset has been on the map for centuries as the last oasis of any consequence to be encountered when travelling down through northern Africa. It is the largest established community in the entire Hoggar region, and in fact there is nothing to compare with it along the wandering route to the south until well into the deserts of the Niger Republic. Even now it is the official Algerian Customs post, in spite of the several hundred miles that separate it from the border.

One of the distinctive landmarks in the area of desert surrounding Tamanrasset is a solitary mountain, named Pic Laperrine. General Laperrine was a French Saharan soldier who pioneered a good deal of the military manoeuvres in southern Algeria, especially in the pacification of hostile tribes. He was also a pilot and in 1919 set out to be the first man to have flown right across the Sahara desert. Though very successful as a soldier, he was less fortunate in the air and had to make a forced landing outside Tamanrasset, having intended to reach Timbuctou in Mali. Neither he nor his friends were killed but they had no accurate way of judging their position. Nevertheless, despairing of any help arriving from outside, the next day they set out on foot, taking all the supplies of food and water that they could carry, and walking in a direction which Laperrine had calculated would perhaps lead them to humanity or a well. After two days they had to confess themselves lost, and, realizing that it would be folly to continue, they retraced their steps to the aircraft, arriving back four days after they had first set out. Laperrine lived for nearly two weeks more, growing ever weaker, before he had a sudden haemorrhage and died, a victim of the desert in which he had spent many years of his life, endlessly striving to win the mountain-dwelling nomads over to accept French rule so that the Saharan peoples could live together in peace. Had he but known, a mere five miles from the aircraft in the opposite direction was a functioning well with plenty of clean water. His fellow-travellers were found near the aircraft after his death, still alive but all of them bordering on insanity.

The mountain, which beams hot and red in the last rays of the evening sun, was named in his memory and now presents itself as a challenge to professional mountaineers. Several years ago we were driving through this region when an expert Belgian climbing team was attempting one face: they had started out before daybreak to avoid the heat of the sun for the first stage, since the sun in these circumstances can so rapidly sap the energy of the most rugged and hardened climbers. We spoke to members of the ground crew, who were in radio contact with the climbers, at about midday, by which time they had covered approximately a quarter of the route up the rock's sheer surface. But the climbing was very hard and the men were already reporting great fatigue. We heard later that they had spent the night on a ledge barely wide enough to support their bodies and been forced to return the next day. Laperrine's Peak was not to be conquered easily!

We had been passing the Peak that day on our way up to Assekrem, amidst some of the most spectacular and awe-inspiring mountain scenery in the whole of Africa. We were driving with one of the Little Sisters of Jesus, an order of nuns who have a base in Tamanrasset, and who – in the case of this branch of the Sisters – have dedicated their lives to the Tuareg; they also have a mountain retreat near Assekrem where one or two of them spend about six weeks at a time, living in simplicity and solitude, before returning to the centre at the oasis. The centre consists of a few rooms built around a courtyard, including a chapel, a work-room, and a room for visitors, always calm, spotlessly clean, and cool, where Tuareg nomads turn up at all hours with any problems they might have. The Little Sisters try to teach them straightforward principles of cleanliness, and help them with everyday cares that trouble them, but never try to convert them to Christianity in spite of their own fervent faith.

We were also taking up some food supplies on that occasion, to leave in their secret *cache* together with two plastic jerry-cans: a special request, since they are strong, light and practical for donkeys to carry, filled with water from the *guelta* some miles away. The reason for the location of the retreat, and indeed for the centre at Tamanrasset, is to perpetuate the worthwhile work that was started at the beginning of the twentieth century by Father de Foucauld. Charles de Foucauld's early life, as the Marquis de Foucauld and a member of the French aristocracy, was far from humble or selfless: he was rich, debonair, and ruthless, and has been described as a worthless, wealthy playboy. He became a dashing, Devil-may-care soldier in

Tuareg men participating in traditional dance at Djanet

A Targui of the Hoggar saddling a camel near Tamanrasset

the Hussars, and was then assigned to do a reconnaissance of Morocco in 1883-4. As a safety measure, he disguised himself as a Jew, learning Hebrew to substantiate his role. His conscientiousness stood him in good stead, and – to his credit – he accomplished his mission with thoroughness and efficiency. This is perhaps wherein lay the beginnings of his affiliations with north Africa, for not long after he decided to shed his past life and all that went with it, to become a Trappist Monk. Eventually he entered a retreat at Beni-Abbès on the edge of the Algerian desert, which was a stepping-stone to the Hoggar Mountains where he ended his days. He crossed the area between Beni-Abbès and Tamanrasset on foot, a considerable achievement for those days, but he was destined to adopt many other aspects of the wandering nomad's way of life.

The site of Assekrem was chosen by Father de Foucauld for its magnificence and its isolation; one of the highest points in the Hoggar range, it commands a vast and extensive view of the surrounding mountains, particularly dramatic at sunrise and at sunset, or when the full moon's clear beam clothes it all in a steely grey light. Father de Foucauld set about building a Hermitage, consisting of rudimentary living quarters, a simple chapel, and a quiet room separated from the rest for meditation and prayer. Although he lived there alone, he made many friends among the Tuareg nomads who lived in amongst the impenetrable mountains, and came up to see him frequently. Through them he was able to compile his *Dictionary of Tamarshak*, which was published after his death and is still the definitive work on the subject. He also received other monks from far afield, who came to Assekrem for the peace, the beauty and the uninterrupted silence it offered, but it was never his mission to convert. In all the years he spent in the Hoggar, he converted no-one, aiming rather at showing his neighbours 'the way of the Truth', which is the example followed today by the Little Sisters of Jesus, and by a Catholic order of men, one or two of whom are always in residence at the Hermitage at Assekrem to this day.

For a long time there seemed to be a certain amount of confusion surrounding the circumstances of Father de Foucauld's death, the only certainty being that he was murdered. At the time of his death in 1916, the Sahara was a hot-bed of unrest and the French were always striving to 'tame' the native tribes. De Foucauld himself was involved with one of these attempts in 1904, together with General Laperrine, taking part in a successful campaign on the Hoggar. Although the Hoggar Tuareg were to become his sworn allies, there were still other tribes, of Tuareg, Senussi and Arab in southern Algeria, who were not, and de Foucauld to them represented the French – who were the enemy. However, when they attacked Tamanrasset, where de Foucauld was staying at the time, there is reason to believe that their intention was to kidnap the Father and hold him to ransom: his death was an accident on the part of a wild youth. He did have his enemies, however: there were those who accused him of duplicity and spying on behalf of the French by taking advantage of his Tuareg friends. It was also claimed that it was these Tuareg 'friends' who, having found him out, killed him to avenge themselves. In so far as he had passed valuable information to the French about the Tuareg, there is some accuracy in the claims against him, but the informing need not have been done destructively. To give him the benefit of the doubt, the information he gave undoubtedly served to improve the relationship between Tuareg and French in the long run, and it is highly improbable that the Tuareg who knew him would have killed him.

Whenever we are in Tamanrasset we always look forward to calling on the Little Sister's centre, under the shade of the tamarisk trees on the far side of the broad river-bed, where we are always sure of a thoughtful welcome. If all the nuns are pre-occupied we stay just long enough to absorb something of the serenity in the atmosphere they generate, but if not we can talk – a constant delight because we know we shall be privileged to learn more about their lives with the Tuareg. As soon as they come to live in the area, they start to learn *tamarshak* in order to be able to communicate with the nomadic families up in the Hoggar who speak nothing else. As some of the Little Sisters have been in Tamanrasset for up to sixteen years they now speak the language fluently and there is very little they haven't learnt about the Tuareg, whom they have come to regard as their own kith and kin.

There used to be quite a number of Europeans living in Tamanrasset, including an English missionary and his family, but Algeria has started to expel these influences as being unfavourable to national interests. Such personalities as the Italian doctor, however, are granted continual extensions to their permits to stay.

Having left the Little Sister up near Assekrem at the nomadic encampment, their high mountain retreat, we were returning down the circuitous track towards Tamanrasset, past such impressive rock formations as the huge Mount Ilamane, the core of a volcanic mountain, when we were waved to a halt by a Targui. Flustered and short of breath, he had apparently recognized us on our upward journey from an encounter some months earlier, and had now come running to the roadside to waylay us. It was not easy to discover what was on his mind as he seemed unwilling to speak openly – but at last he asked us to join him and his family for tea. Already it was late afternoon as we followed him up the stony valley to his impoverished camp, leaving the vehicle on the edge of the track. His family greeted us cheerfully, inviting us to sit down by the fire over which a cauldron gurgled, while they continued their work: they were packing up the camp in a state of some excitement, but it was not until the third glass of tea had been finished, and all the pleasantries were disposed of, that the conclusions we had been forming were confirmed. Round the back of the great boulder against which we were sitting, was a slaughtered camel. Blood was spattered over the rocks, and the innards had been knowingly divided into the Edible and the Inedible. Its body had been hacked into six separate sections: head, neck, forelegs and chest, ribcage and back – split into two – and the rear quarters. The favour that the old Targui had to ask us was whether we would load the meat onto the roof of our Landrover and transport it to his butcher friend in Tamanrasset. He no longer had the pack animals to carry it down himself, and besides in such weather the meat would have been rotten and valueless by the time he reached the market on foot.

We readily agreed, little realizing what was entailed. The dead-weight of a camel is considerable, and two strong men were required to carry the head alone, all the way back down the valley to the road where the Landrover was waiting. The path was littered with loose rubble and stones, winding around boulders and in and out of steep-sided hollows, none of which was too difficult in the daylight but dusk was gathering and night was soon to have enveloped us. Each section of the camel seemed to weigh twice as much as the last, and a separate journey was needed every time, with only four of us to carry the loads. The rear quarters were the heaviest of all, and with aching arms and backs we were forced to halt every few yards to catch our breath, which wasn't made easier by the altitude at which we were working. We were becoming smeared with blood and grime, but the good-natured boosting that we were receiving from the Tuareg family gave us the encouragement we needed, and the pile of dissected camel carcass on the sand by the vehicle was growing ever greater. A sliver of moon had risen in an inky sky from behind the jagged mountains, known as the Guardians of the Hoggar because their silhouette resembles a neat row of colossal soldiers standing guard over the pale thread of the twisting track. By the time we stumbled up to lay the last section on the pile we were all worn and weary, and we had still to lift it all up onto the roof. We devised a pulley system, and all heaved together, the inanimate wet flesh of the camel glistening in the cold moon-light. As we hauled the last limb onto the platform of the roof, and began strapping the load down, it became evident that we were also going to transport the whole family as well as all their possessions to Tamanrasset. This we were willing to do, but we were afraid that there wouldn't be room and also worried about the rest of their animals. It transpired that all they now had in the way of livestock were six goats and two dogs. The dead camel had been their only one, and by selling it for meat they were virtually surrendering their independence as nomads. It had been too old and frail to sell as livestock, but they had intended to walk it down to Taman-rasset and sell it alive to the butcher sooner or later, had it not unfortunately fallen and broken a leg that morning. They had had to kill the beast, and our arrival was the hand of Allah intervening, as a sign that they were doing His will. The old man admitted then that he was prepared to take a job in Tamanrasset to support his family, and that they had struggled against this moment for many weeks. However, he said, as soon as he had earned enough money to invest in a new camel he would take once more to the hills, and hope that fortune would be kinder next time, and that Allah would send rain. We felt deeply saddened for them, knowing only too well that it was more than likely that he would end his days dreaming of returning to the hills, by which time his children would no longer be nomads at heart.

The oldest boy, who was ten, was delegated to stay behind and mind the few goats while the two dogs – to our dismay – were to run beside the vehicle all the way into Tamanrasset. In comparison to other Moslems the Tuareg treat their dogs with both affection and consideration, bothering to establish a relationship with the animal, and it has been suggested that this might be a hangover from the original pre-Moslem Tuareg customs. The kind of dog kept by the Tuareg is a light-haired lean greyhound-like animal, hardy, always alert and always hungry, but tonight the old Targui told us that the two creatures had eaten from the slaughtered camel and needed to run;

besides, he said dismissively, it was down-hill most of the way, and the air was cool.

Low on its springs, the vehicle rumbled into action, but the track was bumpy and rutted, and before many miles had been covered we had to stop again to change a punctured wheel. Thereafter we drove very slowly, anxiously trying to avoid another puncture as we did not have a second spare wheel. When we arrived, the moon had set and the night was blacker than ever. Pulling up in a wide avenue on the edge of the town, we all wrapped ourselves in whatever blankets and coats we could find, and lay down on the sand to sleep, too tired even to think of unloading the meat that night.

We rose at daybreak and before the sun was up had delivered our cargo in its entirety, bidding farewell to the Targui and telling him to call at our tent on the far side of town if we could help him further. Back at our encampment a man was crouched in front of one of the tents, chewing tobacco. It was a quiet spot, out of sight of any habitation, and we were puzzled to see him. He was a rather dishevelled Targui, and getting on in years, but he struggled awkwardly to his feet and came over smiling broadly: he had passed through the area the previous evening when bringing his goats in from pasture and had noticed our camp was still deserted. When he had seen how busy the town had become in the meantime with the influx of tourists on that morning's flight from Algiers, he had wondered about the safety of our camp. Rather than take any risks, he decided to return and wait for us, although he had never met us. He had waited there all night and was now tired from lack of sleep. It is this kind of brotherliness in the most remote and unexpected areas that we find so touching in the desert people; the old man knew us only by sight, but felt that the arrival en-masse of so many Europeans, being an unknown quantity, represented a threat: he acted as much through instinct as anything else. We offered him some packets of tea for his labours, but he declined to accept any form of reward, saying with dignity as he walked off bent on his stick that one day we might have to do the same for him. We never saw him again.

Although we had not expected to be away for the night, we had not worried unduly about it, having found the local people faultlessly honest. We had seen the first manifestation of this honesty some years previously in that same area, on our return from several days spent camel-riding and exploring in the outlying desert with three Tuareg men. We had a memorable few days, penetrating unexpectedly wild country, the camels picking their way fastidiously over the tricky terrain and along deep ravines, so narrow in places as to prevent us progressing. We had seen very distinct examples of ancient *tifinagh* script engraved on the rocks which the Tuareg had tried to decode for us, we had walked for miles in search of firewood, had climbed small mountains, and had even been swimming. Hidden amongst the steep rocks of the Hoggar foothills, *gueltas* of deep and clear water lie, sparkling and deserted; some, shallow and tapering along the stretches of river-bed, are masked by rich green foliage that thrives in the damp sandy soil, and some, higher up, are contained in dark basins of rock in the mountains, rock washed smooth by the cascading rivers of centuries ago. Hoof-prints of donkeys and camels punctuate the banks, and small brown fish lurk in the shadowy depths. Insects, butterflies and birds abound in the vegetation along the river beds, but at the higher *gueltas* not a living thing stirs. We could swim lazily, cooling our burning skin, then dive to the bottom off the shelves of rock.

By the time we returned to Tamanrasset we were thoroughly acclimatized to the camel saddle, and as we approached the town our Tuareg companions proposed a camel race. Confidently we lined up, the rein that was fastened through the camel's nostril held high, bare feet in position on the back of the camel's neck. The shout went up and we all moved forward. A camel is never in a hurry, and so needs to be bullied furiously into running, by swishing the end of the rein onto its hindquarters and prodding its neck with both feet. Once the momentum builds up, however, the camel seems to enjoy the challenge, and the difficulty is in persuading it to stop. The faster it runs the less comfortable it becomes, as, unlike a horse, both the right legs move in unison, and both the left, thereby creating a very uneven and ungainly movement. When the race was over, the member of our party on the friskiest camel was nowhere to be seen – his camel had bolted and no one had noticed in which direction. We were in a wide clearing encircled by clumps of rock, and for a fleeting moment our friend was seen, as his camel fled across an open space between the rocks. Rider's arms and legs were thrashing the air in a desperate attempt not to be thrown, while his charging mount seemed bent on throwing him. They disappeared as quickly as they had appeared, but one of the Tuareg, a young man known as 'Petit Mohamed' (partly to distinguish him from all the other Mohameds, and partly because of his lack of height, more remarkable in the Tuareg than in other people) had leapt onto his camel and set off in pursuit, his robes billowing out behind him, and his leather crop flaying the flanks of his camel. We waited and waited, sitting in the sand as the sun sank and the shadows of the rocks elongated across the clearing. When they finally emerged, our poor friend was very tired and badly shaken up, but by then so was his camel. The two camels and two riders approached us soberly and calmly as though nothing had happened. When they dismounted Petit Mohamed at once produced a bulging leather wallet obviously full of the over-sized Algerian bank notes, which had apparently fallen from our friend's pocket and been spotted by the sharp-eyed Targui about a mile from where he caught up with the rider and camel, who were then flagging a little. At that time he didn't know us well, and could very easily have omitted to tell us he had picked it up if he had so desired. We have found this open and direct honesty throughout all our encounters with the Tuareg and, having learnt to expect it, have never once been disappointed.

As we ambled into the town, the sun dipped over the horizon behind the low, mud-built houses, whose straight rows form the nucleus of Tamanrasset, and we wandered up the main street towards the hotel in which we were staying at the time. In the evening, the main street of Tamanrasset is one of the most memorable sights of the Sahara. At one end is the imposing gateway of high tapering pillars culminating in a sharp point, decorated with abstract patterns in the earth-red mud of their building material, which opens onto a tree-bordered clearing surrounded by small shops and houses. Camels invariably sit under the trees, quiet and immobile in the shade. The avenue extends up through the heart of the town, lined by tamarisk trees with their gnarled trunks and grey-green foliage. Strings of camels nose-to-tail stalk idly down the middle of the road, laden with hay-bundles, vegetables or firewood, and led by a young Targui, still unveiled. To an observer, however, it is the population that provides the interest: it seems that at sundown all the male Tuareg turn out, dressed in their clean, flowing embroidered robes and tightly arranged black cotton head-dresses, to parade the streets, stopping to talk to each other, or striding purposefully along, three or four abreast – creating a slightly formidable impression, since their height is accentuated by their garments. Before we became well-acquainted with individual Tuareg people we found it very difficult, when wandering in the streets, to recognize the men without staring rudely, as the only part of the face visible is the eyes and bridge of the nose – the rest being masked behind all the folds of black – and as the rest of their clothes are all so similar as to be interchangeable. Even now we are sometimes accused of 'walking in a dream' as we fail to acknowledge someone we have met.

The head-dress of the Hoggar Tuareg differs noticeably from that of the Aïr, in that the material is so placed as to concentrate the bulk of it into widening the overall shape, in effect making a thick and heavy brim, whereas the Aïr Tuareg fold the material round to make a high, flat, slightly pointed area above the forehead into which they incorporate their religious charms or *gri-gri*, leaving sufficient material to have a loose end flowing from the back of the head. The subtleties of donning the *taguelmoust* can only be appreciated to the full by the Tuareg themselves, but, as was pointed out by Lord Rennell of Rodd in 1926 in his book *The People of the Veil*, no other people in the world are known to have clung so tightly to their traditional dress as the Tuareg. Their conservatism in this respect certainly adds majesty to their stature when compared to other men, and their elegance is enhanced by the loose clothing over their long, lean and supple bodies.

The hotel to which we repaired after our camel trek was called in those days the Hotel Amenokal – which is the Tuareg word for Chief or Sultan. It has since been renamed the Hotel Tin Hinan, after the legendary Berber Princess. Some claim that she was the ancestress of the Hoggar Tuareg, from whom the present-day Targuia, or Tuareg woman inherits her status in the society. Princess Tin Hinan is supposed to have been exiled from her native land of southern Morocco, for reasons unspecified. She then travelled south-eastward, alone but for her faithful lady-in-waiting, across the mountains and vast empty desert plains as far as the village of Abalessa. Here she is said to have settled, and eventually to have borne sons, who lived in Tamanrasset and began the Hoggar Tuareg people. It is also said that the word Hoggar (or Ahaggar, as is the alternative spelling) is derived from the sons of Tin Hinan; the literal meaning of the word is 'pride', or 'the proud', and it is said to have been applied first of all to these brothers with a Moroccan Berber Princess mother, who arrived in Tamanrasset and were strangely aloof and disdainful towards the local people. We have never heard any mention of who fathered the proud sons of Tin Hinan. For many years this tale was bracketed under the heading of 'Legend', but in 1926 a team of French archaeologists happened to unearth a tomb in the village of Abalessa which contained not only the skeleton of a female body, but also an interesting collection of personal trinkets such as silver jewellery, beads and coins. Her remains had survived through the centuries quite intact, and have now been transferred to a museum in Algiers, where they have been reconstructed as they were discovered, together with all the trinkets. All that can be said of her skeleton is that it had once belonged to a tall and slender woman. In the light of this discovery, there is clearly a lot more historical fact behind the myth of Tin Hinan than had hitherto been supposed, but it is nevertheless probably incorrect to connect her in any way with the origins of the Tuareg.

In view of the romantic story, the hotel named after Tin Hinan in Tamanrasset hardly does justice to the lady, being neither romantic nor particularly well-managed, but this is a familiar complaint with hotel accommodation in the Saharan oasis. There are exceptions, of course, of which Timimoun – north of the Tademaït Plateau – is one, and Djanet another. The hotel at Djanet has coped more intelligently than most, by housing its guests in *zeribas* or grass huts, with an electric light bulb, cement floor, blanket-covered walls and a communal wash room with showers: simple, basic, functional. Hotels of the traditional format – such as the Tin Hinan – fail through being unable to function in the way they were built to function: taps and wash-basins in each bedroom are impressive until it is established that either they don't work, or else they over-work and flood the room. All this is changing, however. Tamanrasset, like El-Goléa, is taking the obvious step in the direction of the universal hamburger, canned music and purring air-conditioners everywhere, by building its own ultra-modern hotel: bars, night-club, flood-lit swimming pool and dance floor, with its own live orchestra imported to drown the faint and tremulous sound of a flute, or of drums being played in the dark outside to the accompaniment of a soulful song.

The morning following our camel-racing episode, Petit Mohamed was at the hotel early to see if we would like to drive up to his village, Amsel, as there was to be a Grand Fête that evening; he was returning by camel straightaway to ensure that the arrangements were being conducted smoothly, but we would be welcome at sundown. He was excited as he had been away from his village for some weeks and had heard little news, and he assured us that the fête would be a great celebration with music and singing and Tuareg dancing, a big bonfire and bowls of *cous-cous*. We were delighted and accepted gladly, agreeing to leave the hotel in the late afternoon.

The journey took us along the route southwards, and then branched off to the right along a rough track for many miles, upwards into the mountains, a track strewn with boulders and rarely travelled by any vehicle. Darkness had fallen as we went lurching and lumbering up the track, and we decided we must by now be near to the village and that it would be wiser to walk. We parked and set off on foot, seeing an outline of small houses on the black horizon towards which we walked. Knowing it could only be Amsel, we were mildly surprised at the lack of firelight, or of any sound, concluding that the festivities could not have started in spite of the lateness of the hour. A dog could be heard to howl mournfully, starting off a chain reaction. The valley echoed with the haunting wail of dogs, and we hurried forward feeling strangely uneasy. In the village there was not a soul to be seen; some of the doorways were outlined by a dim candlelight glow from within, which indicated only that the place was not abandoned. We tried calling out Mohamed's name into the night air. A child began to cry somewhere and then running footsteps approached us. It was Mohamed; he had been waiting to hear the sound of the motor and was puzzled at our arriving so quietly. Behind the anonymity of his veil, we could see signs of great strain on his face, and asked at once what was going on. His sad eyes were lowered for a moment and then he told us that there was a terrible sickness. Since he had been away seven young children had died and there were others desperately ill, including his own little daughter. We asked whether the doctors at Tamanrasset had been up there, to which he replied that they had, but always too late to save the sickening child, and the injections they gave seemed to have no effect. He asked us to go with him to his house, and see his daughter. As we walked solemnly through the complex of silent houses, here and there a muffled sob could be heard, and coughing. We were remembering now how rigorously and strictly the officials had inspected our cholera vaccination papers when we had arrived in Tamanrasset, asking stern questions about the validity of the certificates, though we had not had any interest shown in them in any of the other oases. When we had pursued it by querying whether there had been any outbreaks of cholera, we were told that the inquiries they were making were 'simply routine: no cause for alarm', which at the time we had taken at its face value. We were now beginning to suspect that they had had every reason to check our papers; but if that were so, why had there been no scare locally? We were mystified by the attitude of the authorities.

Our brief visit to Mohamed's little house was very distressing. Outside the door a child lay on a rug, wrapped in a heavy overcoat. Her father picked her up and carried her inside where she whimpered weakly. She was about six years old and even by the light of one candle we could see that she was desperately ill. She shook from head to foot, teeth chattering, yet her head burned and glistened with tiny beads of perspiration. She was emaciated and light to carry. Mohamed's wife sat in the middle of the room watching us quietly, not accustomed to strangers but caring only about her child's well-being. When asked she told us that the girl had had an attack like dysentery for the last two weeks and had lost a lot of weight. She was now incapable of eating, and would only take sips of water or tea in her half-delirious condition. Mohamed was beside himself with anxiety, pleading with us to do something to save his child. Nothing within our power could have helped the girl, except an offer to drive her and anyone else in the village in need to the hospital in Tamanrasset. Mohamed and his wife talked in low tones, at last agreeing that that was the best thing, although they didn't seem altogether happy at the suggestion, perhaps troubled by an innate mistrust of medical men.

One of the prehistoric cypress trees that have survived at Tamrit, on the Tassili N'Ajjer

A prehistoric painting, on a very small scale, from the Tassili N' Ajjer

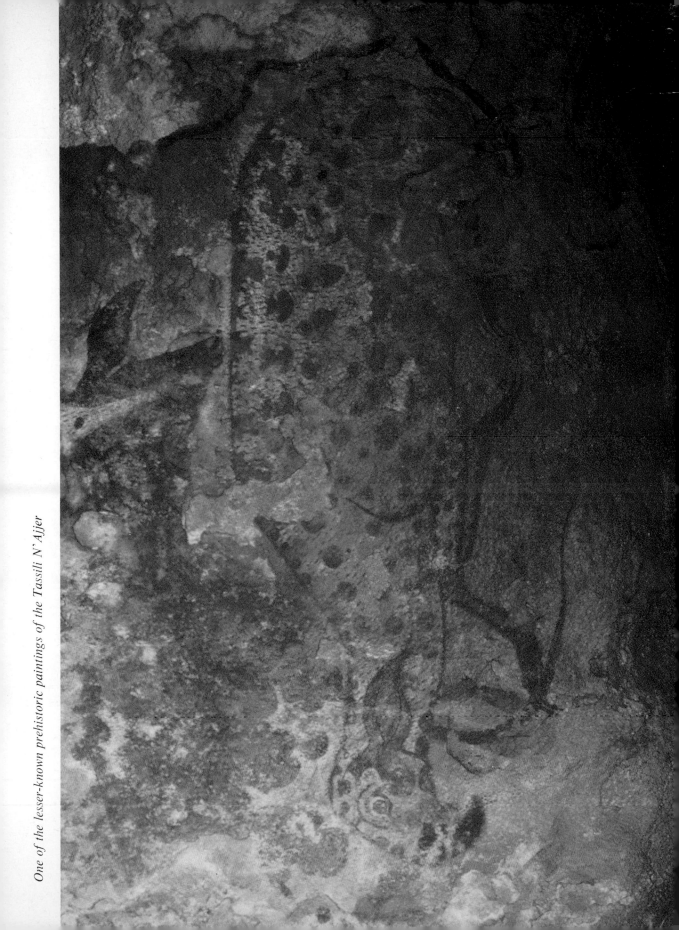

One of the lesser-known prehistoric paintings of the Tassili N'Ajjer

A typical well in the Agades area, with water being drawn by an ox

We all left his house, his wife rocking the child in her arms and stroking away the perspiration from her brow at intervals. Mohamed had two smaller children who weren't there, having been banished to a grandmother as soon as sickness had descended on the household. While Mohamed went the rounds of the silent village to see whether anyone wanted a lift down to Tamanrasset for the hospital, we returned to the vehicle to wait. As we passed through, we saw a group of men were now seated around a flicker of flame in the clearing at the centre of the village, brewing tea. One came over to us – Mohamed's brother, who had spent the last few days with us in the desert – and we were asked to have tea. Few times have we felt more depressed amongst the Tuareg than then. As we sipped tea seated on the coloured rugs they had spread on the ground, Mohamed's brother told us of their homecoming: they had all three trotted enthusiastically into the village only to find, as we had done, no one about, no children playing or women laughing. They had dismounted and run to their respective homes, but it had been worse for Mohamed with his young children: he couldn't believe what had been happening, and was angry that he had known nothing of it, had been amusing himself with us. Now he came up with his limp daughter cradled gently in his arms. No one else wanted to take their children to the town. They were all going to observe the will of Allah: if help arrived at Amsel, that was a different matter. We began to have an inkling of the sort of problems the local doctors were up against. Carefully we handed Mohamed his child once he was safely seated inside the Landrover, and proceeded down the precipitous track once more. It was a wordless journey, the doom surrounding the Tuareg man and the young girl communicating itself to all of us. When we rattled back into the town everything was shrouded in darkness, including the hospital, whose doors were locked. We found a soporific night-watchman who, after interminable explanations on our part, showed us through a side door and into a long tiled corridor from which doors led to sleeping people. A young nun – one of the *Soeurs Blanches* already encountered at El-Goléa – fluttered into the dark corridor in her voluminous white gowns and switched on a weak light. No words were wasted: she agreed at once to take the little girl, assuring us that the formalities could be carried out in the morning. There were no raised eyebrows on her part at the hint of cholera, but neither would she comment on its likelihood, saying simply that there had been some cases of it. We were none the wiser but were reassured by her calm competence. Mohamed had never been into the hospital before and was clearly disconcerted by the prospect of abandoning his daughter to the hands of complete strangers. However, the nun promised to watch her all night and was regretful that he was not allowed to stay with her too. He said he would collect us from the hotel, just a few steps along the main street, in the morning, because he would need help if there were forms to be filled in. Dejectedly, we all retired, he to relations on the edge of town and we to our rooms to sleep fitfully, awoken constantly by horrifying dreams of plague and disease, and by the startling screams and protracted moans of cats fighting in the yard.

The next day was violently windy and overcast, and the dust churned up in the atmosphere to obscure the sun. Mohamed was rousing us long before the hospital

would have opened so we persuaded him to take some coffee and some bread. When
we trooped into the hospital, the nun had gone, but a young French doctor had seen
the girl and told us to take heart: she was not as serious a case as some they had
received lately. When asked what the trouble was, he changed the subject and asked
us to go and register the child at the Reception desk: she would be there for a few
weeks at least, but there was an eighty per cent chance of total recovery. We visited
her with Mohamed every day, while we were able to: an impersonal little being, in a
white cotton night shirt and between smooth sheets for the first time in her life. She
was nearly always in a restless, fretful sleep, sometimes waking and gazing dully about
her, unaffected by the alien environment, her eyes expressing no interest in anything
at all. This was her condition when we left the area, but we had asked a friend who
worked at the post office next door to the hospital to check up on her and send us a
report on her progress, since Mohamed wasn't able to write to us himself. Some
weeks passed before we heard that the girl had been discharged and had returned to
her village with Mohamed, having made a full recovery, but he stressed how lucky
she had been as there were other children who had died in hospital. We read in the
Press of scattered outbreaks of cholera in Algeria, but it will never be known if this
was the disease that had struck the people of Tamanrasset. We were especially
thankful that Mohamed's daughter had survived hospitalization, as we were aware
that if she had not we would have been partly blamed for having instigated it.
Although the Tuareg are now outwardly beginning to accept modern medicine,
especially in the case of those living in close proximity to centres like Tamanrasset,
they remain instinctively suspicious and it will be many decades before they are
finally convinced of its merits.

In spite of his preoccupation with his child's health, Mohamed had been unnecessarily concerned that he had not provided the hospitality he had promised us
at Amsel. No amount of assurances would put his mind at rest, so we were very glad
when our post office friend, a young Algerian named Taib, informed us of an
evening of folk-lore that he had heard about and that we could all attend. As we
thought, Mohamed at once saw this as a compensation for the evening at Amsel and
ceased to worry. We held no high expectations of the evening, as we had so often
found that something had happened to prevent the participants from turning up;
in this respect we had not been the least bit disappointed at Amsel, only extremely
sorry for the reasons why the fête was cancelled.

Taib's information was vague, but he said he was convinced it would be worthwhile. We met him outside the post office when he finished work, as he had invited
us to have an early evening meal at his house before the folk-lore started. Since our
arrival in Tamanrasset we had seen a great change in this man and had wondered
more and more what lay behind it: he was thinner, more subdued and looked
unwell. During dinner, of an excellent *cous-cous* cooked by his neighbour's wife, it
emerged that since our last time there his wife had left him, returning to her parents
in the north of Algeria with their two young children. She had been unable to support
the quiet life in the oasis after two and a half years there, and had fled back to the

big town she was used to. Taib, always serious and earnest by nature, had been prepared to throw up his job and flee after her, but when he went up to Constantine to arrange things he discovered she had already found another man. Taib was destroyed by this and felt his life was over. For six months he had barely eaten, living on milk and cigarettes. Even the night we were there he talked and smoked throughout the meal, never touching the good food.

Most of the top personnel of the post office, the bank, the *Sous-Prefecture*, the hospital and the *Gendarmerie* are men imported from the larger cities of northern Algeria, to spend a restricted number of years in the small oases of the Sahara. In general they resent the lack of diversion in these places, but now and again we have met men who thrive on its tranquillity, most of whom are sensitive people like Taib. More often than not, the married men leave their wives back in their hometowns, visiting them every few months on leave, but Taib had thought, somewhat idealistically, that he should not be parted from his family, but that they should live together. Having failed in this theory, he felt his whole philosophy had been undermined, but would hear no hint of criticism of his wife's behaviour, taking all the blame on his own shoulders and consuming himself with self-doubt and recrimination, asking himself over and over again during the long sleepless nights what he should have done differently. He stayed in Tamanrasset and very slowly his wound began to heal as he began to come to terms with himself, swearing all the while that he would never subject himself to the pain of being a husband to any other woman.

The folk-lore he took us to watch was taking place in the high-walled courtyard of a local restaurant in a corner of the market square. By now we had heard that the dancers and musicians were a team representing the nation in a large-scale folk-lore festival being held in Mali. They were all Tuareg, and this evening was their dress rehearsal or final practice, before departing southwards the next day, so we guessed we were to witness something special. The small scruffy courtyard was lined with the chairs from the restaurant, the glow from whose door and window supplied the only source of light. When we entered through the metal gate in the high wall we saw first of all an instrument resembling a wooden xylophone, beautifully made and about five feet in length. Behind it a man was seated, his head tightly swathed in gleaming black cloth, with the two batons for the xylophone poised in his hands. There were four other men, tall and somewhat sinister-looking, standing in the shadows, and a fifth kneeling over a drum with his ear pressed to the taut skin while he tested it with his fingertips. He had hand-made drums of various sizes about him and several sets of sticks. Behind the two musicians stood another in a pure white *taguelmoust* distinguishing him from his fellow-performers. They were all relaxed, apparently waiting. The 'audience' consisted of the restaurant staff (a one-eyed chef and two shambling waiters), the late-night clientele, to be found in there every night of the week drinking mint tea, playing dominoes and surreptitiously dipping into a flagon of wine under the table, and ourselves. We sat down, hoping we hadn't missed anything, and the chef, feeling in an indulgent mood now that the harrassment of his day was over, brought us all a glass of coffee.

Seconds later the kitchen door opened again and two more performers emerged, stunningly clad in black, white and red, swords swinging at their sides. There was a murmur of appreciation and immediately the musicians started up, engulfing the night with a flow of rippling notes and the throb of the drum's reverberating beat. As the dancers walked slowly and rhythmically into the middle of the courtyard, it struck us that we had never before seen such tall and imposing Tuareg figures, and had never seen them dressed with such care and precision: the black *taguelmoust* was wound intricately around, each tiny pleat perfectly placed, so that even the limited space around the eyes was covered. The forehead was masked in a V-shape that came down between the eyebrows where it was met by the cloth folded over the nose, so that the only parts of the face visible were the two separate eyes, outlined by triangles of pale skin, and flashing with animation at the sound of the music. We have never before or since seen the *taguelmoust* so precisely arranged as to make a division between the eyes over the bridge of the nose, and were aware that this was a symbol of the Tuareg's nobility and superiority to other tribes, as well as a very distinguishing feature. Amongst a variety of African folk-dancers, however exotic, colourful and gloriously decorated the other competitors might be, none would compare with the Tuareg for the awesome impression they created on the impact of their first appearance.

Once assembled in a line in the centre of the courtyard, the six dancers began clapping their long hands in a particularly resonant way, moving their brightly sandalled feet in unison, and looking directly ahead all the time. They all wore swords, and the two criss-crossed in red braid – the latecomers – were at either end of the line. The music was rising and falling, telling the dancers what to do, and as the drum-beat came suddenly crashing and pounding into the foreground, the dancers separated and each in his turn enacted a complicated, rapid step involving a low twist of the body and a stooping, sweeping movement as they spun around, now brandishing their swords above their heads in a wild yet controlled arc against the starry sky. As each Targui performed his individual piece the others danced around him in perfect time, moving with a wonderful grace and freedom, and using their long slender limbs to their utmost advantage. Being rehearsed and polished, this dancing was unlike any other we had seen; although we had often found the spontaneous dramatic and moving, this was unequalled in our experience, both visually and with regard to the perfect synchronization of the musicians. The Targui in the white *taguelmoust* had been standing erect between the drum and the xylophone, clapping and occasionally uttering a shriek of encouragement. He now stooped to pick up a long flute carved in wood, which he placed to his lips from beneath the white veil. Taib whispered to us that the white veil indicated that he was playing the part of Evil, and that when he danced he was the symbol of everything evil in life. The flute, carrolling the notes clearly and sharply, signified a progression in the dancing: the six men divided into two lines of three, face to face with the two decorated in brilliant red in the middle. One side picked up shields from the ground, the heavy Tuareg shields of polished hide, and a new dance started, with each team of three moving as one against the other team, employing exactly the same gestures and movements: one the aggressor and one the defender. Swords banged lightly against the shields, and the actions began to accelerate: those with the shields were on their knees, arching backwards, shields high against the aggressors who stamped and hissed, stabbing the sand around the half-prostrate men; then shields were thrust forwards, and aggressors leapt back, the dance quickening and subsiding, but performed with such co-ordination and fluidity of motion as to be always captivating. For such tall men their agility was surprising, as was the way that their dress was never disarrayed. The dance of the crucial battle was developing: roles were exchanged, swords were being ceremoniously hurled to the ground, and shields discarded. One by one the dancers were fading into the shadows; the Evil spirit had appeared fleetingly on the scene, but now sprung into the centre, whirling and spinning in a maniacal dance, his white masked head swooping and diving against the darkness of the courtyard, his feet never still for a moment. Then the final duel began to take shape as the white spirit tremblingly hovered in the background, responding to each clarion note of the xylophone with every nerve in his body. The two last dancers were the two with scarlet braid, both wielding their swords until one plummeted through the air in a flash of sharpened steel and its owner was pinioned to the ground. The hero was uttering strange sounds, shaking his shoulders and head viciously, threateningly, at his victim over whom he now loomed. The victim was writhing, squirming, to the trilling music, and then the white spirit again sprang to the fore. Xylophone quietened and low drum beats boomed out into a magnificent crescendo: the victim was still; the white spirit danced a frenzied dance around the hero who ceased to shake and tremble and began a jumping, stamping dance that led the two of them out of the light and into the obscurity of the shadows, to the accompaniment of the drum's last dying rumble.

We were all left breathless after this demonstration, realizing how forceful the Tuareg must have been in real battles, and incredulous at their power to dance it out with such strength and feeling. Never had we expected to be involved in so unique an experience. Unnoticed by us the music had attracted many more spectators, and the small courtyard was now crowded with people pressed against the walls. It was pleasing to note from the faces and the applause that the local people had found it as enrapturing as we had. The dancers and the musicians were now tired after their vigorous performance and sat down to enjoy glasses of hot sweet tea. The crowd dispersed, it being very late for the Tamanrasset population still to be about in the streets. We went over to look more closely at the musical instruments, whereupon two of them took up two sets of xylophone hammers and began to play a complicated duet for us. They were relaxed, playing beautifully and at length, even though both had been dancing all evening; they weren't even the official musicians, but they told us that all their roles were interchangeable, they worked so closely together. Before we had a chance for further discussion, they said they were departing to sleep. We left together as they were also staying in the hotel for that night. As we walked through the silent and deserted arcades of the market, the flute was produced and its soft clear notes drifted around us. We stepped into the street, bright and silvered in the wash of moonlight, and wandered up between the tamarisk trees, following the haunting flute music which was unspoiled by any other sound in the silent time of night. We wandered right through the town, entranced by the melody and the scented night air that stirred the leaves above our heads.

We were never to hear of this troupe again. We can only hope they did as well as they deserved in the Mali festival, as there can be few Tuareg alive who could do justice to their tradition in the same way. It would have been a fitting tribute had they been recognized at Mali, for, without any conscious effort to maintain it, the traditional folk-lore of the Tuareg could fast become extinct.

It is in Tamanrasset and the Hoggar region generally that we are made the most aware of the threats to the Tuareg's existence. Many have already suffered the degradation of surrendering their traditions, their way of life, their entire philosophy, but the sacrifice has in each case been essential, induced by the unrelenting drought and the resulting horrifying poverty. It is now forseeable that the mountains will become devoid of nomads, goats and camels; the entire Tuareg population will be forced to come down to the township of Tamanrasset or the outlying villages, to live like every other tribe in a drab uniformity ill-suited to their culture.

III. The Tassili N'Ajjer

III. The Tassili N'Ajjer

The Tassili N'Ajjer, whose name means literally the Plateau of the Goats, is a high plateau of 7,000 feet, stretching across south-eastern Algeria towards the frontiers of Libya in one direction, and towards the farthest reaches of the Hoggar Massif in the other. The two mountain ranges almost touch in a savage, alien world of arid plains, steep crevasses and mountains of grey stones and tumbled boulders. The plateau is attainable only by foot in most parts, but over the last twenty years Djanet, the oasis at the base of its southerly edge (known as Fort Charlotte in the days of the French), has developed dramatically: from a sleepy, insular oasis peopled only by the necessary military, gendarmes, customs men and officials in general, together with a great number of Tuareg nomads in the palm groves, it has now become a flourishing tourist centre, with a tourist plane from Algiers every week and a rapidly expanding hotel, bar and restaurant complex.

The Tassili is composed partly of spectacular and extraordinary rock formations, partly of deep, craggy ravines in which pools of water still lie, and partly of endless tracts of desolate and bleak desert whose plains are strewn with shiny rocks and boulders, interlaced with pale sand. The total area of the plateau is roughly equivalent to that of France, yet the only inhabitants of this rugged and inhospitable environment are several hundred sedentary and nomadic Tuareg.

Along the floor of the now dry and sandswept *wadis*, amongst the labyrinth of rock formations on the southern edge of the Tassili, there still survives a string of large and stately prehistoric cypress trees, some with trunks of up to twenty feet in diameter – a weird phenomenon of a lost world. The mighty trees present a picture of unreality in such a parched and inanimate landscape, and the explanation of their

49

survival from prehistoric times, and through such a drastic change of climate, lies in the extent of their roots, which have penetrated deeply into the ground to obtain sufficient moisture, and in the nature of the wood itself, which is of such density and durability as to withstand attacks from insects and from fuel-gathering nomads. The latter are always in desperate need of wood to build fires on which to cook, but have only just begun to acquire the necessary metal implements to tackle larger trees. Inevitably, the fine cypresses now bear scars, but they have reached such dimensions as to be much less vulnerable than any younger trees.

The Tassili holds a wealth of unique prehistoric art and artefacts, scattered over hundreds of miles on the irregular surface of the plateau-top. When first discovered, the paintings in particular were surprisingly distinct. It has been said that these paintings and engravings, dating back as far as 8,000 B.C., were created by the ancestors of the present-day Tassili Tuareg, but this seems unlikely. It is doubtful that the Tuareg lived in the Sahara so long ago, and the figures depicted do not on the whole indicate any aspect of the Tuareg culture. The theory that is now becoming regarded as the most plausible is that the ancestors of the Peulh people were the rock artists of this part of the Sahara. The Peulh are to this day nomadic breeders of cattle and their herds bear a strong resemblance to those depicted in the prehistoric paintings. The painted human figures, too, are generally more Peulh in character than Tuareg. The one question that cannot be answered, however, is not who did the paintings, but why they were done. It has been suggested that when the environment became less fertile with the gradual change of climate, and there were fewer wild animals to hunt as well as less vegetation throughout the year, the cave-dwellers were prompted to start a simple form of farming and rearing stock to survive. Once dependent on the weather for the success of their harvest, superstition and an awareness of the possibility of a higher being – a God – could have begun to creep into their consciousness, which would have inclined them to worship, involving many different forms of ritual, from decorating themselves and dancing, to sacrificial slaughterings. This could also have involved painting on the walls of their caves.

Alternatively, they may simply have painted for pleasure, to pass the time of day, or to tell a story in pictures which we are not equipped to interpret. It is more feasible on the whole, however, to give the paintings symbolic or spiritual significance as an explanation of why so much effort was invested in creating them.

At the better known sites, which are still used by nomads from time to time, there are instances where nomads of recent times have tried to copy their predecessors with drawings of camels and men; the results are incomparable with the prehistoric paintings, being crude, badly executed and completely lacking in any artistic merit, all of which is predictable. No one will ever wipe away the mystery that surrounds the question of how the primitive artists came to be endowed with so much talent, and what it was that motivated them in their painting and laborious engraving.

When climatic change began to affect the habitat of the Tassili drastically, the population was forced to move southwards in search of better pasture. The Sahara, whose very name means 'desert', had been a fertile area, rich in vegetation and wild-

An impoverished Tuareg tent, with enamel pots, a wooden pestle and mortar, a gerber suspended from a trestle, with a stone quern for grinding corn above it, and all the normal trappings of a nomadic family

A Targuia sings and drums, captivating the onlookers who clap their hands in accompaniment and join in the chorus

A representative array of the nomadic Tuareg's worldly goods, balanced amongst the branches of a tree to prevent damage from animals or sandstorms

A gathering of Tuareg, showing good examples of some of the typical hairstyles

life, including such animals as elephants, giraffe, rhinoceros and an abundance of fish, but it was now becoming dry and windswept. The once fast-flowing rivers, deep and wide, now no longer flow at all, but the sheer courses still cut as clean a scar through the volumes of rubble and rock as they did many thousands of years ago. When the rivers flowed, they provided a vital feature of the prehistoric landscape, and today it is along the top rim of the steep stony banks that many of the decorated rock shelters are to be found – shallow caves eroded by centuries of blasting from the sand and wind. Their floors are still frequently littered with charred bones, fragments of flint, potsherds and stone implements.

In the paintings evidence survives of the use of boats in the Tassili, indicating that the rivers must have been a major means of communication – which is quite a thought in view of the parched and silent terrain there today.

As the flow of the rivers grew more and more feeble, so the inhabitants gradually shifted to more attractive lands, possibly through the extensive mountains of the Aïr. Only three years ago the skeleton of a prehistoric domesticated cow was unearthed by a British team of archaeologists in these mountains, found about a foot below the surface, and dated at approximately 20,000 years old: could this also relate to the cattle-breeding Peulh people?

Until the discovery of the rock art on the Tassili in 1933 by Lieutenant Brenans, a Frenchman stationed at Djanet, it had been generally accepted that the extent of human life on the Tassili had never been any more interesting or remarkable than that of the present day: a scattering of nomadic people scratching a meagre existence from an unyielding environment. In this context, therefore, it is easy to appreciate what a wondrous discovery it was – a whole world unfolding, and the story of an era long dead being disclosed, to the delight of prehistorians everywhere. Even now, forty years later, 'new' sites are still being discovered.

The first time we encountered the truly nomadic Tuareg, whose lives have been practically untouched by the fast-changing world beyond their horizons, was in late February some seven years ago. We had embarked from Djanet at the base of the Tassili, with two camels and a Tuareg guide, to walk across the plateau and search for further unrecorded prehistoric sites.

The days were hot, dry and invariably windy, while the nights were very cold at an altitude of 9,000 feet. The terrain varied from echoing surfaces of grey rock, the floors of deep ravines worn smooth by tons of fast flowing water but now long dry, to soft engulfing sand, interspersed with a profusion of rubble, gravel and broken boulders which proved none too easy for the camels to negotiate. Where either pasture or water was plentiful, a break in the march was called for to allow the camels to replenish their reserves. On such an afternoon we had chosen a sheltered camp beneath the towering cliff that formed one bank of the river-bed we were following, and had led the now unladen camels to a *guelta* or water-hole, necessarily hobbling their forelegs to prevent them straying too far. The kindling that had been gathered over the last few miles of the march was now unbundled and a small fire lit to make tea. Since the first day away from Djanet, we had adopted the lifestyle of our guide as far as possible – it obviously being tailored to the environment – and a significant aspect of this was the tea ritual. It was rare ever to drink while on the move, however parched and leathery our throats and tongues became, but on stopping tea was a priority: first attend to the animals, then light a fire to heat water. The tea drunk by the Tuareg is an imported green tea, sometimes supplemented with aromatic plants picked locally. Coloured enamel tea-pots are used and normally a battered kettle. Three brews of tea are made and tradition insists that all present drink one small glass of tea from each brew, which are made progressively sweeter and weaker. The three glasses drunk are to oneself, to the assembled company, and to Allah, respectively. However ragingly thirsty we were, we were always surprised to find how successfully the thirst was assuaged by these sips of sweet tea – more effective by far than the pints of cool lager we dreamed of from time to time!

After tea our guide spread himself out in the shade of a rock to sleep, carefully covering his face to thwart the indomitable flies, while we wandered off to explore, equipped only with waterbottles. At one time this river-bed had roared and swirled with cascading waterfalls, for we had steep hundred-foot drops to negotiate along its course, at the base of which clean-sided bowls still retained rainwater, and even some fish, in the heavy shade of the cliff. After scrabbling for several miles along the river-bed, which then sprawled onto a wide plain spotted with dried undergrowth and boulders, we had paused by a *guelta* to rest and cool our feet when we noticed some movement amongst the boulders. Anything animate is of immediate interest in this lifeless terrain, as it is a possible indication of humanity. We picked and stumbled our way over the plain, and were approaching a herd of goats when a bent figure, cloaked in black, peered around a rock in front of us. We had surprised each other, but her expression was of disbelief rather than fear: this we later discovered was accountable to the fact that never in her long life had she seen Europeans before. She was gnarled and very wrinkled, her small eyes narrowed against the hard glare of the white sun, but her feet were nimble as she darted between the rocks, stopping now and again to scrutinize us suspiciously. Not wanting to add to her discomfort, we stayed very still, trying not to look intimidating in any way, and her distrust seemed slowly to ebb. She came over to us and we all shook her hand, muttering such greetings as we had learned in the Tuareg language: '*Matulit*', and replying '*Il-herras*'. We parted, and she scampered away like a girl, hurrying back with the goats to her camp to tell her family of her experience. The sun was low and the black mass of rock before us, into which our ravine cut an elongated vee, cast a cold shadow over the plain. By the time we had climbed back up the river-bed – wishing we had the skill of salmon in surmounting the high steps that punctuated its course – our guide's fire was an orange flicker in a dark and silent world, towards which we gratefully plodded, footsteps resounding and echoing up and down the corridors of rock. The guide was clearly excited by our story of the old lady on the plain, and said that next day we would visit their camp if we could find it.

When the Tuareg are tracking, two things are remarkable: first, their concentration and alertness which, though always with them when they are travelling, now

Tuareg girls drawing water from a crude well in a village in the Aïr Mountains

Victims of the Saharan drought. The desert is strewn with hundreds of such corpses, amongst which human bones are also to be found

Debris left by the French military in the Arak Gorge, contributing to the ruination of the environment

Dune formations on the Ténéré Desert

takes their full attention so that there is none of the usual chatter and song; and secondly, the expertise they demonstrate by finding small signs even on a rocky surface to indicate the passing of a herd. A recently snapped twig is spotted some yards away, animal dung is examined to gauge its freshness, footprints in the sand are closely observed, ashes of a dead fire are turned and smelt, pasture is watched for signs of having been torn or nibbled. As well as learning all these natural signs, the Tuareg are also taught to leave messages along the path, if one exists, for the next Tuareg who passes to read. To us these seem to be a crude arrangement of stones in the form of an arrow or a cross, but their juxtaposition conveys much more to the Tuareg, who can even tell you which tribe or clan of the Tuareg people left it there.

As we steadily and watchfully led the two camels forward, following the guide who was hopping hither and thither in search of clues, we became aware of a mounting tension generated by him. From the break of day he had been unusually preoccupied and had awoken early to catch the camels, returning to the camp with them in record time for us to load. Normally we all helped to load, but today he had had to devote more time to his appearance. We were intrigued to see him grooming and attiring himself in clean white robes, and new sandals (the Tuareg sandals are always fastened together sole-to-sole when they are made, so can easily be recognized as never having been worn), finally embarking upon the ritual of the *taguelmoust*. This is the well-known Tuareg veil, which consists of at least six metres of a fine cotton about one metre in width; generally it is either black or white, although the shiny indigo-dyed cloth which is responsible for the naming of the Blue Men is still often worn, especially for important occasions or festivals. Except on the first day we met him in the Mayor's office in Djanet, we hadn't seen our guide veiled as he apparently didn't regard our company as worth the bother, and there had been no other company for days and days. His everyday appearance was usually shabby and tattered – bare-headed and bare-footed, finished off with an ancient cotton pullover, a mass of holes, over his baggy black 'Moslem' trousers. But as we watched him carefully organising his head-gear now, we witnessed a transition from an urchin-like scare-crow to a distinguished and almost noble-looking man. His veil had been assiduously pleated, and placed immaculately over his head, around his head, once across his face and under his chin, increasing in width each time he wound it around again, eventually tucking the frayed end out of sight. One of the most distinctive features of the Tuareg is the fact that the veil is worn by the men, as in most other Moslem societies it is the women who are veiled. The Tuareg women frequently do not cover their heads at all; a black shawl is worn over the shoulders and lifted over the hair for warmth, or across the face only as a protection from the sand in a sandstorm. The reason why our guide was going to such lengths on this occasion was that he knew we were liable to meet a group of Tuareg nomads that day. Tuareg men are never seen by their own people unveiled, and thus much pride would be at stake if our guide should be caught out. We understood that he wasn't sure which tribe of Tuareg we would meet, which explained why he was paying such attention to detail.

Meeting strangers involved protocol and formality.

We had set out before the sun had risen, but now it was reaching its height and we walked on our shadows in silence. The camels maintained an even, unfaltering pace as ever, the first being led from a rope through a ring in its nostril, the second tied to the first by a rope around its lower jaw. The guide, like all the Tuareg, never seemed to tire but strode on relentlessly, his eyes searching the horizons, penetrating the parched long grass of the undergrowth and the chaos of fallen rock amongst the mountains. One or two trees were growing and we were once more on sandy ground when he pointed out that the animal tracks we had been following were not only very recent but included those of camel, donkey, small children and adults, super-imposed in a confusion of churned sand leading around the base of a rocky outcrop. Seconds later the cries and laughter of small children reached us, and a lean, pale dog streaked around the rocks towards us, ears sleeked flat against its head and hackles up; our guide shouted to it and it stopped, and slunk away. A large, smiling woman then appeared, accompanied by a younger woman nursing a baby. They were heading towards a pool with empty goatskin water containers or *gerbers*, talking loudly and laughing, and didn't at first see us. The three of us fell back while our guide walked forward to greet them.

Amongst desert dwellers and nomadic peoples everywhere, time is never short; conversations need not be rushed, and exchanges of all kinds take place at a leisurely pace. When the Tuareg meet, whether or not they are known to one another, they unhurriedly ask each other how they are, how their families are, how their camels are, and many other questions concerning health and well-being, to which the reply is always, regardless of circumstances to the contrary, 'Very well, praise be to Allah'. Some time later, for example, we were present at a meeting in the Hoggar Mountains between two Tuareg men who had grown up together, one of whom had just lost his wife, who had died in childbirth three days earlier. On encountering each other, the habitual exchanges took place, but they had been speaking for more than half an hour before the death of the woman was disclosed, despite repeated tender inquiries from the friend.

During such communications, an interesting hand-touching procedure takes place: outstretched right hands meet flatly together, slide away and fold shut just as the fingers lose contact with each other; the hand then touches the heart and is stretched forward again. Depending upon the length and depth of the relationship, this can be repeated seven or eight times, but strangers generally touch hands three times or less. At meetings like this the Tuareg speak quietly and gently to each other, and even give an impression of shyness as they finally lapse into silence.

After our guide had been talking with the two women for several minutes, a group of men came over and the women wandered off towards the *guelta* to fetch water, continuing their happy chatter, while the men began to greet us all and welcomed us to their encampment around the corner of rocks. The camp consisted of five or six tents, low on the ground but capacious, made from leather skins stitched together with thonging and stretched over an arrangement of poles. They had all been erected in the lea of the mountain and had an enclosure at the entrance, crudely marked out by sacks of dates and millet, camel saddles and rocks heaped on top of each other, forming an irregular low wall. Once we had unloaded our camels we were invited to sit under a tree, not a stone's throw from which sparkled a long shallow pool where a couple of donkeys drank and an arthritic old woman was scrubbing a printed cotton dress. As she turned, we recognized her: she shrieked with laughter when she saw us, and skipped towards us dripping with water – much changed since the day before. Thereafter, whenever she caught sight of us during our stay there she giggled and spluttered with amusement.

By now the guide was chatting unreservedly with his companions, but it was some time before we discovered that these were all his brothers and cousins, and that in fact almost everyone in the encampment was related to him in some way. An older and most dignified Targui, swathed in a black veil and blue cotton robes, had summoned a young boy to fetch kindling and sticks. A fire was built in the midst of our circle and tea made. The Tuareg, as always when on their best behaviour, never revealed their faces even to drink tea, but lifted the veil with the left hand, inserting the small glass behind it in order to sip the tea. This behaviour is maintained for eating as well, the lower face never being shown in any kind of formal atmosphere.

An important piece of news soon emerged from the talk around us. In two day's time the annual sacrificial feast, the *Fête de l'Aide*, would be held – a Moslem festival at which a sheep or goat is slaughtered and eaten by each family, with much celebrating. As we hadn't anticipated being anywhere but in a rock shelter, alone with our guide and two camels, this hadn't been a consideration until now, as we found ourselves suddenly in the midst of a thriving community. We were all invited to stay at least for the feast, if not for a week, and we readily agreed. It was to prove to be an unforgettable experience.

After all the glasses had been washed meticulously – always by the man who had made the tea – and wrapped in rags for safety, a few more pieces of wood were added to the embers, as the sun's rays carried no warmth this evening. The sun was sinking slowly, but not in the vivid explosion of reds and purple-oranges we had grown to expect of the Saharan sunset: this evening it was a citrus disc in a greying sky, barely casting a shadow. Pulling their goat-hair cloaks and blankets closely around them, the Tuareg explained that we were in for a windy night, and that the bad visibility was simply the sand and dust in the atmosphere, stirred, lifted and borne by an already determined wind.

The thought occurred to us that this might be a night for our tent – hitherto little used – and this was seconded eagerly by our guide, who dearly loved our tent and obviously longed to show it off to his relations. With its zips and nylon fly-sheet, collapsible poles, fixed ground sheet and metal pegs it was a slight embarrassment to us in such an environment, but to the Tuareg it was a beautiful and priceless object which they not only erected for us but laboured to surround with a low stone wall for protection.

For the first time there were no stars, and no moon cast its silvered spell on the night-scene. No one had slept but now people could be heard; the wind carried voices away so that a shout became nothing; sand was swirling and stinging in the air and people were running in all directions, like a ship's crew when a storm is imminent, fastening, securing, gathering up and roping down. The children, faces obscured against the cruel blasting sand, cried forlornly, groping their way like blind men around their enclosures, until they too were scooped up and placed inside a tent home. The panic amongst the animals was the cause of the men's anxiety. They dragged the goats, bleating and frightened, to shelter where they were bound together by their horns. The donkeys, unnerved and lost, cantered frantically around, wailing and groaning as only a donkey knows how, but the camels were the worst worry, being further from the encampment in search of pasture, and not easy to find even in stillness and daylight. Now the imprint of a hoof stayed on the ground for seconds only, before eddying sand obliterated it. Everybody was up, and we all searched and called, stumbled and faltered, peering despairingly through the angry night for the silhouette of a camel. On sighting one and seizing it, a rope had to be threaded through its nostril ring, or round its lower jaw, and it wouldn't willingly co-operate, its instinct being to stand motionless, eyes closed behind a fringe of long curling lashes, and wait for the sandstorm to subside. But untended it was in danger of tripping over and crashing to the ground, breaking vital bones and dying an un-necessary death. This was the concern that drove the Tuareg on, for hours into the night, and on, even towards the weak dawning of day, before each beast was ac-counted for. As the daylight began to penetrate through the howling and churning fog-like air, we crawled back to our tent, aching and spent, eyes raw and burning from exposure to the elements, to find the tent flattened and half-buried by sand. The struggle to re-erect it should have caused the Tuareg a flutter of complacency – theirs had all withstood the battering.

Somewhere the sun had risen and the light had turned to beige as we lashed the final guy-rope to a tree, evocative of shadow-puppets as we staggered and pranced in the tearing wind, finally creeping into the relative calm of the interior.

Despite the raging weather, by mid-morning the tent was too hot, too stifling to tolerate without any air filtering through it: we lay inert, wet with rivulets of per-spiration that made scars in the coating of sand on our skin. The sand was all over us, having permeated several layers of clothing, and this, we learnt, was just another Saharan condition. The rest of the camp was quiet, but for the persistent roar and rip of the wind, and the intermittent groans of a camel. We left the tent and blundered once more through the storm, towards the pool to fill our waterbottles, and then upwards towards the mountain, figuring that the flying sand had to have a ceiling. Struggling up sheer boulders and heaps of rock, eyes and mouths now full of sand again, our progress was very gradual in the turbulence, but eventually we reached a point where there was wind without sand. We climbed on, out of sight of each other but calling out at intervals, until a flat ledge lay before us, out of the wind. Eventually the three of us were there, and there we stayed for the rest of the day, listening to the wind, watching the sky and the sandstorm below, and sleeping spasmodically at last.

Unlike some of these storms, which can last for over five days without interruption, this one was mercifully short-lived, and by the afternoon was already diminishing in tempo. As we descended through the now still air, the camp was unrecognizable, as if cleverly camouflaged to match the environment, coated in blown sand which gave everything in it a dead uniformity. People were emerging from their tents, like animals awakening from hibernation, ready to sort out the chaos caused by the storm. A young woman was already pounding millet with a tall pestle, lifting it above her head and thumping it down into a wooden mortar, the sound of the rhythmic banging carrying down the valley in the quietness.

Our own tent stood limply now, sagging from its poles but unharmed. Such equipment as we had been unable to store inside had to be unburied and cleaned, and this we were doing when we were joined by a group of Tuareg for whom we lit a small fire and brewed tea. Their chatter was animated and excited, concerning the events of the last twenty-four hours. Apparently, little damage had been caused, but all the animals had not yet been found and our guide had last been seen some way off, searching for his second camel. We had wondered about him, and now felt concerned; after a brief debate one of the men agreed to come with us to look for him. As we set out, carrying only water bottles, the air was becoming clearer and an early half-moon appeared behind the mountains in a transparent white sky. The floor of the desert was like a beach just after the tide has gone out – washed smooth and not scuffed by footprints. We headed in the direction in which he had last been seen, along a narrow sandy *wadi* between the mountains. Now and again our companion shouted out as we walked, to be met only with the echo of his own voice, and silence. Not a sound stirred the air.

After two hours we found ourselves on the rough surface of a low plateau which afforded a long view through the last shreds of daylight. Somewhere below we heard a fall of stones, then again quiet. Just as we decided there was nothing more we could do, the Targui called out. He was straining to see in the twilight and as we, too, looked, we saw the figure of our guide – tall and pale amongst the rocks – approaching us wearily. As soon as he was within earshot he began a series of shouted remarks, to which our companion responded similarly. As we met, we could see things were not well, and in a short time we learnt that one of our camels had fallen into a crevasse during the storm and broken its neck. Our guide had found it jammed in the rocks, head wrenched backwards, which is where it had died. The guide was very grieved and could hardly even bear to speak of it. He walked ahead of us all the way back, wordless and worried, through the heavy black night between the high walls of rock.

The camel plays a very large part both in the life and the economy of the Tuareg: a man's wealth is only assessed in terms of head of camel, and of course the nomads depend heavily on their camels, for prestige and transport chiefly, but also for milk, cheese, butter and even meat. To lose a camel is considered a tragedy, and certainly in the encampment that night there was a very morose atmosphere. After sharing an especially gritty bowl of *cous-cous* everyone went off to bed, without the normal laughter and lively exchange to which we had grown accustomed to falling asleep.

On the day of the feast our simple breakfast of dried fruit, tea and biscuits was interrupted by our guide telling us that our best clothes were necessary, which placed us in a predicament. 'And trousers are not suitable for a woman today' he added, presenting a further problem, though at last we were able to produce a cotton dress, albeit crumpled, from the bottom of a rucksack. From the *wadi* on the edge of which we were camped, we had been watching a steady stream of people from the encampment slowly progressing across the wide stretch of sand, all decked out in their finery. The men, who had preceded the women, were wearing very carefully arranged head-dresses of smooth black cotton, and flowing white embroidered robes over wide black trousers; they all wore the same type of red leather sandals as those that our guide had put on for our arrival at the encampment. The women had clean, fresh, embroidered loose blouses and shawls of black, blue, white and gleaming inky purple, over long black skirts twisted around their middles. The silver ornamentation in their ears, around their heads and on their hands sparkled and dazzled in the morning sun. The Tuareg jewellery is extremely distinctive and very beautiful, and most women have a personal collection, however humble. For festivals, nothing is left unworn, so that men and children alike have rings, armbands of stone or religious amulets. It is common practice to wear leather pouches as necklaces, which are meant to contain an extract from the Koran and therefore be a protection against evil spirits, but for festivals the more exotic and colourful decorations are worn.

As the entire community snaked its way in a disjointed line to a remote rocky outcrop, we realized that they were paying a ritual visit to their improvised 'mosque' – a clear patch of desert marked out with a square of stones which has probably existed and been used by nomads for centuries, as have the many others that we encountered on the Tassili Plateau in the course of our wanderings. The men drifted back first, and separated into groups around the tents, the elders making tea with exaggerated pomp and ceremony, while the younger men went towards an enclosure of stone in which goats bleated pitifully. Four goats were dragged over to the rocks, and a Targui ran up to us to borrow one of our crude scout knives, as there was to be a sacrificial slaughter. They all became highly excited – issuing commands and shouting loudly. We were told that 'the woman must leave' but the other two were to stay and help by holding the goats down.

By now the women had returned to the camp and were busy around their tents, rolling *cous-cous* through fine sieves and pounding dried dates with a pestle and mortar. Once well pounded, the dates were split onto a square of cloth and the stones were meticulously sifted out (and put aside as a rare treat for the camels). The remaining dry substance was then thrown in the air and caught again in the cloth, the light wind catching the 'chaff' and blowing it away, so that what eventually remained was only the dry flesh of the dates. This was then tipped into a wooden bowl of sour camel-milk and stirred for about an hour. The end result was very much like sweetened yoghourt and very good.

A pot of spicy vegetables with a lot of tomato paste (from tins bought in Djanet) was boiling over a glowing red fire which a small boy was feeding with dry camel dung – very good slow-burning fuel – on top of which an enamel bowl with a perforated base was placed and filled with the *cous-cous*, by now rolled into tiny balls, where it had to steam for at least an hour in the vapour from the vegetable sauce. All the women were unusually locquacious and stimulated: on a normal day they tend to be very capable, but serene, and almost subdued at times; now the gaiety was infecting everyone.

Back at the scene of the slaughter, the goats had had their throats neatly cut while being held over a rock very firmly by three people, so that the blood drained away at once. Each goat was then beheaded and very skilfully skinned, by making a neat incision in a rear leg and blowing air between the skin and the flesh, so that the poor dead beast blew up like a balloon but was then easier to skin. This process prevents undue damage being caused to the skin itself, which is at least as precious to the Tuareg as the meat, having a long life ahead of it as a *gerber* or water-carrying vessel. *Gerbers* are patched up and repaired for years before they are abandoned; they are particularly valuable as they can be slung on the side of a camel for travelling, or between two branches of a thorn tree in camp; with the steady seeping of water through the skin, and evaporation in the air, the water inside is kept relatively cool, and yet is still easily poured out of the hole at the neck. The orifices are all bound up with a kind of sisal rope, which is made from a coarse growing plant gathered locally. We first saw this rope being made at another camp on the Tassili plateau. An old man sat down in the sand with a pile of the coarse weed beside him, and deftly began to feed it through his naked toes, twisting it with his hands, stretching it, spitting on it, and muttering either blessings or curses on it, until he had a length of thick, tough and efficient rope. The adroitness with which his feet manipulated the twine was a sight never to be forgotten.

Once the sacrificial goats had been skinned, they were dismembered and the wet ribbons of flesh were laid out on a rock to dry in the sun, so that they could be stored rather than eaten at once. All the flies in the area made a bee-line for this rock, of course, but the Tuareg seemed quite unperturbed by them. The livers, kidneys, hearts and so on were wrapped in suet and prepared for the spit-sticks, with a scattering of hot chili powder (and, inadvertently, sand), whereafter they were passed to two young boys who tended the fire over which the sticks were balanced, periodically turning the sticks until the suet had melted and the delicacies were ready to eat. The men were now seated cross-legged on large woven rugs spread out on the sand, and the women came forward bearing the steaming pots of *cous-cous* drenched in vegetable sauce, one of which they planted in the midst of each group, together with a bunch of spoons. Choice morsels of meat were offered to each person and the serious eating began. For the Tuareg, any variation in their habitual diet is welcome, but to have such good things as this was indeed an occasion. We ate in silence until everyone had had his fill, when the women removed the rest of the food. A very large enamel mug of murky water was passed around before the meal was officially over, and everyone stretched out in the sun while yet another brew of tea was prepared, and the women retired to the shade of the tents.

We slept all afternoon under a leafless tree, feeling strangely unwell, to be wakened at dusk by the sound of beating drums which drifted over from the direction of the tents. We wandered across and found that all the men were sitting around as ever, talking and laughing tirelessly, but all the women and girls had gathered further up, in an enclosure outside a tent, and now shrill voices were accompanying the drum beat. A young woman approached us and invited us to join their party, apparently disregarding the fact that some of us were male. The day was fading fast, and the stars were already visible above. The only light came from a small fire beside which the old lady we had originally met minding the goats was crouched. She was cradling a baby under her arm, as did many of the older women while the mothers worked. Tonight their jewellery reflected the hot glow of the embers and their faces shone warmly. Three older women were seated cross-legged in a row with young girls beside them: this was the 'choir'. The rest of the women formed a circle, seated around the edge of the low stone wall enclosure, clapping their hands to the rhythm of the drum beat. A young girl seemed to be chief drummer, and we could tell she was extremely practised – her hands, fluttering like the wings of a panic-stricken butterfly, barely stopped for a second. The squealing sound we had heard was uttered by the old woman in the centre of the line, who was the wife of the head of the community: she maintained a high piercing note, making her tongue tremble against the roof of her mouth to create a warbling effect – reminiscent of the Red-Indian war cry. At once the rest of them joined in as a preface to a song, a song probably invented by one of the members of their group, and almost certainly concerning love. To an unaccustomed ear the sound was both doleful and monotonous, but we have since learnt to appreciate the subtler innuendos. The words are generally very touching and sentimental, and the lead-singer has to be very experienced to remember all the words of the verses of the many varied songs and at the same time be able to sustain the tone.

We had been observing this party for quite a while before we saw, almost obscured in the shadow of the large tent behind, two seated figures, very straight-backed and completely motionless – so still in fact that our first impression was that they were some kind of effigy. Our attention was drawn to them by the fact that any woman who wandered into the group went first to these two figures and greeted them. It was impossible to tell in the feeble light whether they touched them, shook hands with them or how they paid their respects, but it was clear that the two figures played a major part in the ceremony, although we couldn't even determine whether or not they were both female. We wondered if it was a coming-of-age ceremony, or even a wedding – but these were questions which were not to be answered for a long, long time. It was years later that we discovered, at a similar celebration in the Hoggar mountains, that the seated couple were a young man and his future wife: their 'engagement' coincided with the festival and was therefore celebrated in this fashion.

The drumming, the singing and the clapping built up in tempo: the atmosphere

Djado - the deserted and ruined village

A Tebu woman at Djado

was alive with excitement, and perspiration glistened on the faces of the singers. Suddenly the drummer girl asked us to play her drum – a fine pottery-based one with camel-skin stretched tautly over it. There was an awkward moment, but happily our friend had apparently had some experience, so was able to save us some embarrassment! He only had to perform for a few minutes, because the Tuareg ladies found our westernized attempts hilariously funny and begged us to stop . . .

Meanwhile, the male sector, still grouped on rugs around a guttering fire, were equally absorbed, but in a macabre lizard-baiting ceremony. This involved laying a large half-dead lizard on its back on the embers of the fire, and watching it undergo the agonies of being burnt alive. We were powerless to intervene effectively, but our protests were at last heard when they began a playful tug-o'-war with the wretched reptile. They resignedly threw it into the dark surrounding shadows where we glimpsed it staggering away in a daze to a more peaceful sanctuary. The pleasure of the evening seemed to have been in no way marred, and the talk and laughter rang out for many hours. This we regarded as the sign of a successful party, since it was quite without any added stimulants – except for an occasional wisp of tobacco which was either smoked or chewed with relish.

When we finally returned to our tent to crawl into our sleeping bags, it was with a warm sense of gratification. Even in such an outlandishly remote region, a group of people who had minimal contact with the world outside had been able to take a day out from the routine and arduous tasks of their everyday life, and simply enjoy themselves, calling on all their resources to make the occasion festive.

The next day was spent negotiating the terms on which our guide would be prepared to accept the responsibility of transporting his cousin's young camel to Illizi, our destination. Unfortunately, it was not even broken in and was therefore useless to us as a pack-carrying animal. The guide knew the terrain ahead very well, and knew the difficulties we could encounter with fully matured and reliable beasts, let alone with a young, frisky one. The cousin ultimately agreed to accept the full responsibility for any hazard, so it was decided that we would leave at dawn the following morning with the two camels, only one of which was fit to carry luggage. This meant of course that we would have to take turns in carrying our rucksacks ourselves, which would undoubtedly impede our already laborious progress.

At the encampment, daily life was restored to normal and everyone's fine attire had been stashed away again in the leather bags and wooden boxes so rarely opened. The women were preoccupied with domestic chores, cleaning the ashes and goat droppings from the sand-floored tents, kneading a flour-and-water dough to make bread, pounding millet, and stone-grinding corn by hand. There were two kinds of primitive grinders in use: the most usual was simply a large stone with a flattened upper surface over which a smaller stone was rubbed, crushing the corn grains between the two smooth surfaces. The other was more elaborate – a large round stone with a hole worked into its centre, and with a peg driven into its top surface off-centre. The peg formed a handle by which the stone was revolved on top of another smooth stone, while grains of corn were fed through the hole from above. The action of the two stone surfaces rubbing together served to mill the flour, which gradually – very gradually – seeped out of the edges to fall onto a cloth. As with all these mundane tasks, the Tuareg women made them seem effortless, but when we tried even to undertake the pounding of millet that a slight child of not more than twelve years old was working at, we were straining after several minutes. Corn grinding requires considerable strength to be sustained over the necessary period of time to produce enough flour for one loaf.

Our guide was equipping his saddle bags with fresh stocks of dates, dried *cous-cous*, flour, tomato paste, and macaroni, while we painstakingly filled the *gerbers* with water from the pools, a cupful at a time. The pools had been covered with a film of fine sand since the day of the sandstorm, which made clear water harder to collect. Our own bags were easily packed, and we were strapping them up when a young man approached the tent. Since our arrival we had seen little of him, but had noticed him particularly, as he shook hands with his left hand, keeping his right hand out of sight. His mission just now was to get us to look at his right arm. Inside the tent there were no flies, but once out of the breeze the heat was fierce. We rolled back his loose sleeve and were appalled to see a gaping wound above his wrist that was clearly rotten. The flesh was encrusted with poison oozing from the wound, together with dried blood, and flies, while the smell was overpowering – we were afraid this may have been the result of gangrene having set in through neglect. Evidently, he had been badly scalded some weeks previously. Though it was obvious that he was suffering a great deal of pain, having virtually lost the use of his arm with swellings in his armpit and neck, his request was simply that we should do whatever had to be done to prevent the wound from deteriorating. With limited medical knowledge we could only call on common sense, and so set about thoroughly cleaning the wound and disinfecting it. This took over two hours, and revealed an extensive area of red-raw flesh – a deep hole in his forearm. Then there was the problem of hygiene in such a fly-infested environment. We constructed an elaborate protective cage from twigs, adhesive strips of bandage and gauze, which was judiciously fixed to his arm – clumsy but very effective. We gave him penicillin pills to last for a week's course of treatment, and ample instructions about cleanliness around the wound. The perspiration was coursing down all our faces, but our 'patient' had not winced or uttered a gasp throughout the proceedings. His name was Baba, and he will endure in our memories as one of the gentlest, the most courageous and sensitive of the Tuareg we have met. Some fifteen days later we were fortunate enough to run into one of his relations, who reported – we hope accurately – that the arm had been completely cured without leaving any side-effects.

The last vestiges of night still hung in the sky to the west as we strapped the final teapot to the camel and said goodbye to any of our new friends who were up and out already. The guide was energetically and nimbly coercing the wilder young camel into having a noose fitted around its lower jaw, by which he could lead it. Then we were ready, and the bizarre procession across the desert embarked once more in single file. As we left the encampment, Baba emerged from his tent and came to us with a present of a beautiful prehistoric stone axehead, small, smooth and finely patterned. We still have it to this day, though we never saw Baba again.

Walking before sunrise was exhilarating, as we were free from flies and comparatively cool. The sun's appearance over the distant ridge of mountains brought long shadows and the habitual hum of small insects, though the varied and constantly changing scenery we were walking through helped to divert our attention from the latter. There were long avenues of twisted and fallen rock whose floors were silent with soft sand, swept smooth by the recent gales and punctuated only by the even trail of a beetle's passage, leaving a series of tiny indentations in parallel lines, or the heavier tracks of a lizard whose tail would flick up the sand on alternate sides, or the curious flat path of a sand viper. In this world of looming rocks, we would now and again come across a deep pile of sand like a mighty drift of snow, nearly reaching to the highest level of rock, over which both camels found it difficult to pass. We had much pulling and pushing to do, and encouragement to give by way of guttural croaking and hissing. The guide darted off at intervals to pick a plant he had spotted, which may have had any one of several functions. The first time we saw him show any real delight was when he saw a tall flame-yellow plant like a giant orchid growing nearby. Selecting a sharp stone he dug it out, taking great care not to break off any roots, and fastened it to the camel bags. That night we were to eat the roots, cut up and baked under the embers of the fire in the scorching hot sand. Their texture was of potato, but they were very bitter to the tongue, and it took us many days to become sufficiently accustomed to them to enjoy them. At other times we noticed him gathering a small-petalled blue flower which grew intermittently, but it was weeks before we discovered its use, and then only by chance. The guide never intruded unduly into our affairs and certainly did not pry, but even he could not fail to observe that one of us was suffering from a bilious attack one day that necessitated falling behind from the rest of us while on the move or dashing away for cover to one side of the path. We prescribed the usual antidote for this kind of upset, and expected it to be effective within an hour or so; on the contrary, the condition apparently worsened. In the evening the guide stepped in: from a strip of knotted rag he produced a handful of tiny dried flower-heads, smelling sweet and pungent, that he administered with confidence: 'Eat these' he said sternly. Within a period of twenty minutes the condition was cured, and never returned.

Another plant was picked purely for its smell; the succulent leaf had a lasting aroma and the custom was to crush this between the fingers and push it up one nostril, leaving it there until the aroma faded. Again, for a while we found it more comfortable to do without; but eventually we learnt to enjoy it as the Tuareg do, as we began to appreciate the value of anything that enhances the day to day existence, however transient or trivial.

Having turned our backs on the nomads and their encampment, where we seemed to have experienced so much, the next few days were spent walking hard to compensate for the time lost. Our guide was inflexible in his routine for which we were, in retrospect at least, grateful. Each day, after a dawn start, we walked for a minimum of eight hours without a break, and then if the weather was not insupportably hot we would still continue for a further four hours, eating a handful of dates if hungry, and perhaps having a gulp of water from the *gerber*. Had we insisted on stopping for an hour's break at some stage, he would have acquiesced but his silent disapproval was not worth invoking without a very good reason. If we stopped at midday to shelter from the heat we had to unload the camels and give them at least an hour to rest; we would invariably build a small fire, make tea and possibly a thin soup, and then hunt for a patch of shade in which to sleep. If no rocks offered shade, we would cover our heads and sleep in the sun until it was time to continue. We all found it worse starting out for the second time in a day and so adopted a routine for the first few weeks of our trek whereby there were no stops at all; towards the end of the journey, when we were a mere two weeks away from our destination, we were obliged to rest at midday for the sake of the camels, but our guide, too, preferred the unbroken march.

Four days after leaving the nomadic encampment, we had come to the end of another day's travelling in a region dense with massive boulders and hidden shelters, which we looked forward to exploring. The guide had banished the hobbled camels to search for pasture, and was singing a wordless, tuneless song as he bustled about the fire preparing to cook. We had agreed to his doing all the cooking that night as he wanted us to share his macaroni stew, and we therefore spread out to collect kindling and any fuel we could find to keep the fire burning. Fuel was a constant problem in this arid terrain, and sometimes entailed wandering several miles from the camp just to return with a meagre bundle.

As we limped back, separately, we were astonished to find we had company: a nobly attired old Targui on a camel was talking to our guide – who must have had a few minutes' warning of his arrival as he had had time to don a rumpled over-dress and wrap his *taguelmoust* around his head. After we had greeted the stranger, he dismounted and sat with us for tea, and the guide explained that he was the brother of the chief of the clan for the entire area, the Meddak people – or, in their terminology, the *Kel Meddak*. The chief's encampment was a mere ten kilometres away, so we considered detouring the next day in order to visit it. The Targui assured us that our presence would be very welcome, particularly as the youngest wife of the chief was sick and in need of 'aspirin' – the magical cure-all of the travelling European.

The visitor was clearly going to spend the night with us, so we began preparing our baggage as a windbreak. In the act of moving a heavy stone, we disturbed a big black scorpion which raced around angrily searching for the interloper. Even the Tuareg were initially alarmed, but the guide, with a deft twist of his stick, flicked it from its sandy domain directly into the flames of the fire where it died instantly. As it was early in the summer, we had encountered no scorpions until then, and the guide took a delight in recounting his many experiences of them. According to him, the traditional – and infallible – Tuareg remedy for a scorpion sting, is immediately to cut out the flesh into which the sting has been injected, and then, opening the stomach of a living dog or goat with a knife, thrust the wounded part into this orifice; the circulation of warm blood in the animal pumps all the poison out of the system, leaving only a bad cut. This treatment, he said, was also applicable to snake bites. To us it sounded drastic treatment, especially as it entailed sacrificing a useful creature from the camp; we wondered just how effective it was, and rejoiced that we had so far avoided being stung!

The chief of the *Kel Meddak* was living in an encampment of only three tents – far smaller than the one we had left several days earlier – and as we approached towards midday the following day, he came forward to meet us. His head and shoulders were shrouded in a black cloth so that we couldn't see his face, and a child led him by the hand. 'The sun blinds his eyes' said the brother who had ridden beside us all morning. The chief's name was Hammah, and he greeted us all joyfully, inviting us into the shade of his tent.

Amongst the Tuareg it is quite permissible to have as many as four wives, following the dictates of the Koran, but it is nevertheless rare to meet a Targui who has taken more than one. In the case of the chief of the *Kel Meddak*, there were two, a tall and dignified middle-aged woman who was seated in the tent working on leather embroidery for a camel saddle bag, and a very young woman who had apparently just given birth to her first child. The community consisted of not more than a dozen people altogether, including a crippled child who wore an unchanging expression of tranquillity, smiling with his beautiful dark eyes, though he could do no more than sit in the sand at the entrance to his father's tent, watching his brothers and cousins racing up and down the sloping rocks. It looked as though he was the victim of polio. After the initial introductions and courteous exchanges, our guide asked us to visit the young wife who had stayed in her enclosure apart from the others. We found her slumped in a corner of her enclosure, faded and drooping like an unwatered flower, with her old mother close at hand. A tripod, normally used over the fire with a pot suspended from it, was now draped with a black cloth under which a six-week-old baby boy lay sleeping soundly, naked on the sand. His young mother was evidently very sick, vomiting every few moments, her face drained of any colour – sallow skin stretched over fine bones. We saw at once that there was blood in her vomit, and were told that she had been unable to retain any food or water since the baby's birth. Deciding quickly that if she was haemorrhaging we were ill-equipped to help her, we advised that she should immediately be taken to the Djanet hospital. To our dismay, this announcement was received as a joke: Djanet was at least twenty days away on a camel, and the woman was unfit for such a journey – and besides, if it was God's will He would make her well; if not, it was His will that she should die. Our reaction was to argue and remonstrate, but they were heedless, adamant. None of the medicines we had with us was suitable for her as nearly everything had to be taken orally, and this she was unable to do without rejecting it straight afterwards. The girl watched us, hopeless and dull-eyed, occasionally forced to smile at our foreign ways and at our clumsy concern for her, which her own people did not manifest in any way. The baby would awake now and again and yell with the gusto and vehemence of a normal, healthy newly-born child, which seemed to underline the pathos of the mother's situation – she was too weak even to lift the baby in her arms. Her eyes, rimmed with the tiredness of days and days without sleep, now echoed the calm understanding and serenity of the crippled boy's, by which we had felt so moved; in spite of the fact that she complained of a pounding pain in her head, she looked as if she no longer experienced sensation of any kind. We left her having failed to comfort her at all, angry and frustrated at our inability to alleviate her suffering.

When we returned to Hammah's tent, he asked us if we could look at his eyes, though he maintained there was no hope for any improvement. It was the least we could do, so we set about it before the afternoon light weakened. When he emerged from the obscurity of the veil under which he had been hiding, we saw that his eyes were tightly closed, the lids glued together by the dried secretion of an infection, which also matted his lashes. Patience, hot water and cotton-wool eventually cleaned all of that, but he was still unable to stand the glare of light when he opened his eyes – the whites of which were excessively bloodshot. More by good luck than good judgement, we had some eyedrops for conjunctivitis with us – one of us having had a mild attack before leaving home. We administered a few drops in each eye hopefully, and then had to do the same for various other less acute eye-sufferers. Eye diseases and infections are easily the commonest Saharan complaint, and wherever we went (or wherever we go now) treatment for eyes is a priority in the medical kit. But at our first encounter with Tuareg nomads we were novices, and certainly had scant knowledge of medicine beyond health and hygiene; the small bottle of eye-drops had to be regarded as gold-dust, and strictly rationed. We promised Hammah a follow-up dose the next evening, and then delivered a pep-talk on Flies Off The Eyes. These nomads had wearied of brushing the flies away, so that even small children were already suffering from severe infection, with up to six flies resting on the eye-rims, aggravating the condition. We encouraged them to wave their hands about their faces all the time, until they too realized that once clean and dry the flies were much less interested in them. The reason why Hammah wore his black tent-like veil had nothing to do with vanity, but was purely to minimize the light that penetrated his eyelids and caused his eyes to hurt. He removed it at night, but even then could not face the flames of the fire.

Before retiring that night we took a lamp up to the enclosure in which the young mother was huddled; the baby was now in the care of his grandmother, who sat cradling him and pushing soaked and swollen millet into his mouth, the milk of his mother having long since been inadequate. The older woman crooned and rocked the baby, but the young mother seemed abstracted and half-delirious. Her temperature was very high and she shivered uncontrollably. We wrapped her up warmly, and tried once more to give her at least a pain-killer that would also induce sleep. Once more it was rejected, and she waved a feeble hand at us to indicate that she wanted to be left alone with her torment. We left her and went unhappily to our tent, where sleep was impossible. All night there were comings and goings, running footsteps on the stones, the sound of burning wood and of tea being made. By dawn we had heard the news that the ill-fated woman had died. Our guide came into our tent and sat with us quietly as the dawn filtered in. He told us that Hammah had asked us to go off for the day, that he knew of a good site for prehistoric artefacts to which he could direct us, and that he would like us to eat with his family that night – after we had given him his medicine.

Without encountering anyone from the family, we made our way out of the camp and up into the rocks behind as fast as we could. It was only an hour's walk to the flat, gravelly plain that had been described to us by means of many sketches in the sand, and we carried only water-bottles, some dates and some cloth bags in which to carry back our findings, if any. We had been told that we would find the plain rich in axeheads and flint arrowheads if we looked carefully. At first we found nothing but a few unrelated potsherds of dubious antiquity in grey-coloured clay, but after several hours, when the sun was reaching its height and we were right on top of our shadows, we began to discover some little broken flints, and then some finer arrow-heads, which gave us the necessary incentive. All day we searched, bent double or crawling on all-fours, now and again joining up to compare findings. Some really fine specimens were being unearthed, and we could happily have continued for as long again, had the daylight not been waning. We slung the bags, now bulging, over our shoulders, and returned to the camp where a fire glimmered as usual. Hammah came running to meet us, waving his long stick about in front of him excitedly. He was in a great hurry to tell us that his eyes were much better, and that he was beginning to be able to see things again when he was out of the sun. In his tent we gave him more drops and were delighted at the rapid improvement: much of the redness in his eyes had cleared, and if he squinted he could see better than he had done for years. He was now in a strangely buoyant mood in view of his bereavement, but we found later that this is usual among the Tuareg: it is not their custom to weep and mourn, accepting hardship and loss of life as the Will of Allah, and only indulging privately in any grief.

Hammah was now making earnest proposals about exchanging his older wife for 'the white woman', which we had considerable trouble in sidestepping; we suspected actually that he was after the eye-drops – which he presumed would be thrown in as part of the deal! – so assured him that we would not leave him until his eyes were cured.

We could only assume that during our absence that day the community had interred the body of the young woman; no one spoke of her and the enclosure had been dismantled. Hammah said they were planning to move on as the pasture in this area was almost exhausted and the goats were no longer feeding well; however, perhaps his wife's death had some bearing on this decision too.

The following morning the improvement in Hammah's eyes was even more dramatic, as was his ecstasy. Before the sun was up, he wandered around unveiled shouting for everyone to admire the beauty of his eyes. Because he seemed to suffer as soon as the sun climbed from behind the rocks, we had the idea of giving him a pair of sunglasses. A simple act, but thereafter we were his Saviours, and lifelong brothers. At about midday he came up to us with a brilliant notion: in return for all we had done for him, he would take us to see some exceptionally large and good prehistoric paintings at a site never before exposed to the gaze of anyone but the Tuareg. We were curious at the description he gave us, of three huge human figures in one cave, and became very eager to start out. He said that that day he was too busy organizing the dismantling of the tents, the packing up of all their belongings and the gathering in of all the animals, but that he could leave his family to continue the work without him the next day, to take us to his secret cache of rock paintings. We were to pack up all our possessions too as we would not be returning to this camp. Our guide was very impressed that Hammah was taking us to these paintings; he told us that the area was known only to the local Tuareg and the caves on whose walls we would see the paintings were used by the *Kel Meddak* as their private winter storage place: if any outsider should learn of its whereabouts all the winter stores would have to be transferred to an even more secluded place.

As we walked next morning we found ourselves becoming increasingly excited and intrigued at the prospect of what we might find ahead of us. The terrain was more arduous than anything we had come across, involving rugged hills and vast rolling dunes. At one point we doubted whether the camels would ever surmount these dunes because even unladen they fell back further at every step than they had clambered forward; they had to be pushed from behind, pulled and cajolled from in front, and even when they managed to reach the summit, we had to stagger back down and somehow convey all the baggage up, the weight of which made this a very slow process indeed. When we reached a certain point, the guide ran off separately with empty *gerbers* to fill up at a nearby *guelta* in the rocks, as water had been running short at the camp and we had left practically without water. Two of us went with him to help carry the filled *gerbers*, leaving the third with Hammah to continue on course with the camels. Unfortunately, the *guelta* the guide had in mind was dry, and so he headed towards a more distant one in which he swore there was always water. Running all the way to beat the fall of night, we eventually found it and began the laborious process of filling the *gerbers*. At half-full, he insisted we must rush back to catch up with the camels or we would never find them in the darkness.

Meanwhile several hours had passed and Hammah wore an anxious frown, worried about the possibility of not joining up with the guide and two men that night. He began issuing orders to chase up towering and precipitous rocks to look out for them, which luckily proved at last to be a worthwhile strategy. After a few minutes' torch-flashing and whistling the two parties again linked up, just before total darkness fell.

Even in the dark we could tell that the place we were going to was indeed very hidden away: we were climbing along a rocky trail, through a sudden valley, and again up until we came to a sheer drop of several metres which we slithered down while the guide led the camels round a gentler route. We seemed to be in a flat space surrounded by mountains, but we were too exhausted to explore, legs aching from the dune scrambling. We gratefully bedded down under a ceiling of brilliant stars with no moon.

The day that followed was one of the most exciting ever for all of us, and it had a very abrupt dawning: we three awoke simultaneously to the cries of our guide whom we heard racing about on the rocks. He brandished a stick and was beating it to the ground as he leapt from side to side, as if trying to strike some creature. By the time we joined him he had hit it – a thick horned viper – and it was sufficiently mutilated to be dying. Once there could no longer be a shadow of doubt as to its lifelessness, the guide stood up straight and proud while we congratulated him. He told us how he had spotted it just after he had finished his morning prayers, and led us to the spot, in the sandy part where we had all been sleeping. On tracing back its tracks through the sand we discovered that the great snake had spent a blissfully comfortable night coiled up at the neck of one of our sleeping bags. The guide was eagerly antici-pating our reaction, and when the horror of the potential danger dawned, he leapt in the air again, but this time with glee – how he had saved us! Bravo! What a trusty guide he was! Bravo, bravo!

Hammah had been absent but now came up through the early shadows of morning laden with kindling and dried grass to start a fire. We were all hungry, so they pro-duced some cold macaroni with lumps of bread soaked in the sauce, and we opened two tins of corned beef, which neither of them would touch, stating categorically that it was made from donkey meat – a strict taboo in their diet; we ate separate breakfasts but they were glad to have some of our sweet, black coffee for a change. By the time we had straightened out our camp and recovered from the snake-episode, it was broad daylight and we could look about. We were in a wide basin surrounded by overhanging rocks, the bases of which formed shallow caves, or shelters. From the ceilings of some of these shelters all sorts of leather sacks had been hung, as well as bird- and animal-snares, camel saddles, a variety of pots and pans, a bundle of tent poles, and so on. The sacks contained dates, millet, grain and even dried *cous-cous*, and were placed carefully out of the reach of any passing animal. Now we understood the logic in the secrecy they had imposed – and even suspected that we were deliberately taken up there after dark, and probably by an unnecessarily circuitous route! Not a stone's throw from the most spacious and, judging from the goat droppings, the most used shelter there was a great fallen boulder, on the side of which we noticed some scratched markings which we were able to recognize as *tifinagh*, the Tuareg writing, though we were not told what it meant. Hammah lead us around the boulder to reveal his *pièce de résistance*: we were facing a wide shallow cave whose exterior formed a wide arc in the face of the rock. As soon as we stepped nearer we saw the amazing paintings of which he had spoken. There were three giant figures of men running, on a larger scale than any of the other human figures ever recorded on the Tassili Plateau, and in an extraordinary style – the outline boldly painted, with a scollop-motif superimposed on the inside of the outline. The mural clearly told a story, for there was a smaller, seated figure in the corner which could have represented a nursing mother, and the male figures (one of whom seemed to wear a beard, to the amusement of the Tuareg) could have been engaged in a furious chase. We were staggered, both at the scale of these paintings and at the condition in which they had survived over so many centuries.

Having digested the impact of the cave, we began delving about on the ground. The cave measured about twenty metres across, and had obviously been used by nomads and their livestock for years: there were charred cinders, droppings, broken pottery and a scattering of small bones, probably from snared birds that had ultimately garnished the *cous-cous*. Once we had penetrated the surface layer, however, we came across one or two fine axeheads, and even some flint. Hammah by now was in a strange mood, fluctuating between severe mistrust and supreme satisfaction at our excitement. But when we produced a camera, there was trouble. No photographs of his private store; no photographs of rocks, or caves or paintings: publicity would bring tourists like at Tamrit and Sefar, the well-known sites on the southern edge of this plateau, and that would be the end of his hiding place and his privacy. On this matter he was inflexible, and we felt we had no right to argue unduly. Hammah said we could spend the whole day looking around, for our own pleasure, but that was that. We must all leave at daybreak the next day.

Once his prerogative had been established, he appeared to relax a fraction, and told us to follow him down the *wadi*. We climbed a smooth rock and then squeezed under another fallen boulder flat on our stomachs, finding ourselves on a ledge in a dark cave. As the light filtered in and our eyesight adjusted, we discerned a decorated wall, painted with peculiar animals. Here Hammah indulgently said we could take a photograph, just one, because no one would recognize the environment; we quickly complied, and the result is shown in this book.

We spent the entire morning investigating this area, and were both stimulated by the wealth of unexcavated territory and frustrated at having so short a time to spend there. Apart from the particular paintings Hammah had indicated to us, there were no other obvious ones, but the large cave was so sensationally different from anything else we had seen that we were convinced it bore some significance to the whole picture of prehistory in that area, and were anxious to relate what we had seen to more authorized persons than ourselves. It was actually two months after our return to Britain before we could arrange a meeting. Monsieur Henri Lhote and his wife invited us to spend a week-end in their delightful house built in the side of a cliff beside the River Cher in France. Lhote is the prehistorian who has undoubtedly undertaken more work on the Tassili paintings and engravings than anyone, and was the first person to organize an expedition specifically to record and catalogue the works of art discovered on the southern edge of the plateau, in the region of Djanet. His book, translated into English and entitled *In Search of the Tassili Frescoes*, gives as much information on the known sites as any other, but Lhote has been criticized for instigating the sponging down of paintings in the interests of his photographs, rather than considering the longer-term interests of the paintings. Although when wet the colours of the paintings are naturally enhanced, each time they are sponged they are fractionally fainter on drying out, and we have observed a progressive

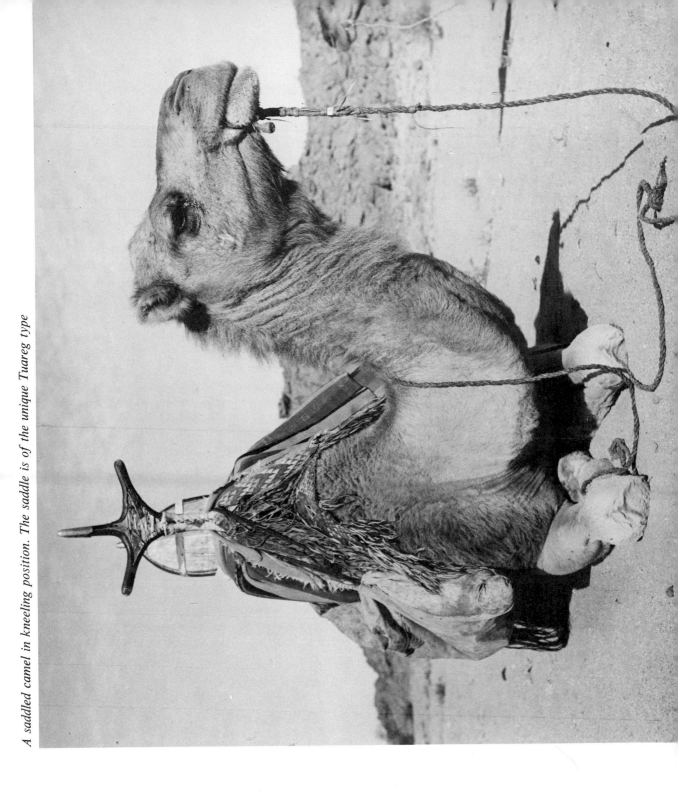

A saddled camel in kneeling position. The saddle is of the unique Tuareg type

A young Tuareg mother claps to the rhythm of song, whilst other Tuareg women watch the drummer behind

A young Tebu woman dressed in the simple clothes of the wandering nomad, her hair arranged in plaits and strands of unplaited hair. Safety pins are highly valued amongst the Tebu and Tuareg alike

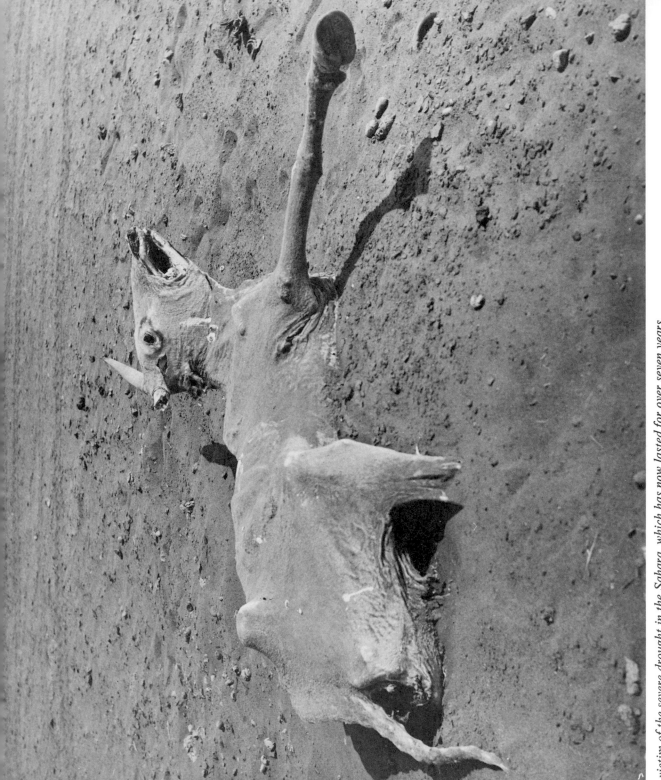

A victim of the severe drought in the Sahara, which has now lasted for over seven years

deterioration in the quality of many paintings. Now that the sites he has popularized have become a strong tourist attraction, measures are being taken by the Algerian government to curtail the actions of visitors – some of whom were going so far as to chisel off sections of painted rock to take home. It is questionable whether these measures have been enforced in time to be fully effective, or whether the rot has already set in and it is too late to save the paintings from the grasping and unthinking clutches of the casual visitor. During our stay with Lhote, he expressed great interest and enthusiasm in the paintings Hammah had showed us, and was excited by the sketches we had made. We explained the situation to him, that the site was not to be made known publicly or developed as a commercial venture, but that a serious scientific expedition could be mounted to record the intriguing and possibly unique figures in depth, and to research the outlying area. Needless to say, no names were mentioned.

Back at the site, we were engrossed in examining the floor of a small cave, sifting the dirt and sand through our fingers in search of treasures, when the guide announced that it was necessary to fetch water from the nearest *guelta*, which was half an hour's walk. We took the camels to have a long drink, filled all the *gerbers* and all had a good wash as it was an unusually large and clean *guelta*, seldom visited by men or beasts, hurrying to return to the base camp where there was so much to explore. On the way back we took turns to ride the camels bare-back – a disagreeable experience as their backbones were much sharper to sit on than they looked. But it was during this wander back through a jungle of rocks that we spied a clay rim of a pot jutting up through the sand. On digging down, an entire pot emerged, packed solid with sand but undamaged apart from a missing handle. Its base was rounded, evidently for balancing in the sand, and we bore it back to the camp ceremoniously, to pack carefully away for the journey. We all doubted the chances of getting it back in one piece but we were determined to try – and not in vain. It exists today as we lifted it from the desert, but we have since learned that it may be a mere 500 to 800 years old – in other words practically brand new in prehistorian's terms, and hardly worthy of a second blink!

Very regretfully we had a last look round the *Kel Meddak's* secret mountain hide-out, trying to register all the details of the paintings indelibly upon our memories. Throughout our time there, our host had never been far away from us, and had surveyed us, hawk-like, from the tops of rocks. Now it was time to part he was relaxed but impatient to return to his family and expedite the changing of camp – but not leaving before he had extracted more promises from us not to speak indiscreetly of his mountain by name, and had escorted us on our way.

Once again we had unexpectedly lost several days of our somewhat haphazard schedule, and the week that followed consisted of quietly trudging across the northerly stretches of the Tassili N'Ajjer from dawn till dusk, in single file, followed by the two camels. The altitude was decreasing as we progressed, and we noticed this most of all at night, as we had grown accustomed to the rapid cooling in the air temperature. Now even after dark the air was warm and sultry; we were aware of many more insects, and passed restless, disturbed nights. During the day we were bothered by tiny flying insects that whined and droned in clouds around our heads without cease, penetrating our ears, noses, hair and eyes, in spite of our efforts to mask ourselves against them. We were constantly fishing these small creatures out of each other's eyes, until it became so intolerable that we swathed our faces and heads in lengths of muslin originally bought to strain badly contaminated water. But in this way progress was impaired as we could only see half as far as normal from behind the layer of muslin. We stumbled solemnly along, resenting being unable to appreciate our environment, and conscious of the fact that our trek was nearing its end. On the insistence of the guide, we stopped at midday each day to rest the camels and to snatch some sleep. The younger camel, which we were simply transporting, had none of the staying power of the other, and would balk at the more difficult tracks and passes, lashing out with its rear legs and roaring dismally. The guide had always to hobble the young camel himself, as her temperament forbade anyone less experienced attempting it; crouched beneath her large frame, he would anchor her head by pulling down the halter and treading firmly on the loose end, and would then scream invective at her as a distraction while his strong, sinewy hands deftly twisted the rope around the forelegs, and unfastened the halter. It seemed to us that this camel was unusually silly, always making life that little bit more difficult for herself, and this impression was corroborated before the expedition was over.

Meandering down the northern slopes of the plateau are wide sandy river beds, converging in places, and flanked by dense green undergrowth. Throughout the year these *oueds* are dry, unless there should be a fall of rain, when – astonishingly – a great surge of water will flow in a mighty torrent, as the ground is too dry, in the main, to absorb it quickly. Though brief, this torrent can be deadly, drowning and destroying everything in its path. Whenever in the vicinity of such an *oued*, the guide would not contemplate camping if there was so much as a hint of cloud in the sky, because of the risk of rain. He said there was never any warning, and that just a short cloudburst could have this result, since all the accumulated water streamed immediately down to the main artery of the *oued*. Although we weren't to witness the phenomenon, we were confronted by evidence of it everywhere along the *oueds*: dry and bleached bones of animals littered the rippled sand in parts, together with the relics of tents (any human bones would have been discreetly removed by passing nomads, who are superstitious about leaving the remains of their ancestors exposed to the skies); in some places the shrubs and bushes of the banks were flattened and broken, or uprooted by the force of the torrent. Soon we were to learn that the danger did not end when the water left, but could linger on for weeks given a certain type of sand composition: the water would render it quick-sand and thus highly dangerous to anything that trod on it. Whenever we had to cross such an *oued*, we would wait at the edge while the guide went to great lengths to map out a safe route, stamping his sandalled feet on the seemingly solid sand to test it.

It was just after midday when we emerged through a tangle of foliage to find ourselves overlooking a washed and gleaming expanse of sand, with a strip of green

The interior courtyard of the fort at Bilma, typical of a desert outpost

A Tuareg family group at Kourboubou

Salt being mined at Bilma

Cakes of salt baking in the sun at Tegguiddan-Tessoum - literally, 'the house of salt'

bordering its far side, beyond which was more desert. We had noticed at once that the sand beneath the bushes was damp, and concluded that there had been a very recent 'wave' of water. The guide ran out to test the way, having agreed that we would rest up for two hours on the far bank in the shade of the undergrowth. After jumping about and racing up and down the stretch of sand, he finally returned to lead us across. We advanced tentatively, he watching every footstep of the camels. The sand seemed firm enough, and we left hardly an imprint upon it. Gaining confidence we stepped up the pace, desperate to reach the far side and shelter from the scorching noon-day sun for a while. Suddenly there was a scuffle and a roar ahead: the young camel was bucking, rearing up on her hind legs in a way we had never seen before, for the hind legs were now foreshortened, embedded in sand and visibly sinking. The guide's face was horror-stricken and he was momentarily stuck for words or actions, until his common-sense took command once more. He yelled for one of us to take the other beast back to the bank, on exactly the same path, while the rest of us went to help him unload the struggling animal that he was trying with all his strength to hold still. The forelegs were now also deep in the quick-sand, and fast becoming deeper with the kicking and protesting of the camel. While we managed to burrow under her belly to unstrap the baggage saddle that was firmly anchored around her girth, the guide somehow managed to wind a rope around one of her bent front knees, knotting it securely before fastening the rope around her jaw, hauling the head down as far as he could, and thereby restricting her movements effectively. Then we were all told to run to the bank for branches, twigs, leaves, anything we could find, and to bring them right back. He was scooping sand out from around the camel's rear quarters, and quickly stuffing the branches we brought into the gap, building a platform under the sand. All the time the camel was very gradually sinking, her body disappearing inch by inch into the silently engulfing sand. We worked furiously, frantically, digging out sand and thrusting in handfuls of foliage and sticks, each single-mindedly concentrating on halting the process of slow submergence, scattering sand in all directions as we burrowed like dogs around the suffering camel. At last it seemed that she was static – but by now only her back, chest, neck and head were above ground. We stood back, heaving and panting, clothes clinging to our bodies wetly. We looked at the guide and he was on all fours in front of the camel, evidently gauging the possibilities of saving her. Crawling forwards he plunged his hand once more into the sand, then the length of his arm. He was untying the camel's knee, and finally pulled out the freed rope, leaping to his feet. Without a word he gesticulated for us to go behind her and lift when he said. He wound the rope around his right arm and looked sharply about him for a foothold. No one spoke, or even breathed, in the tension; terrified that our efforts had been in vain, we stared fixedly at the guide's face waiting for any sign from him. Filling his lungs with air, he suddenly let out a deafening shriek, and he was pulling, straining, heaving on the rope – his back parallel with the ground. Automatically, we had dug our hands underneath the camel's hind quarters and were lifting for all we were worth. The guide's shrieks intensified. The camel moved. We were all crimson, veins bulging and muscles taut. Again she shifted and seemed to subside like a lump of inanimate flesh. The guide was nearing the point of despair and hysteria could be read in the expression of his eyes. He appeared to summon every last ounce of his strength for an ultimate attempt – and with an ear-splitting, unearthly scream he pulled on the rope with all his might. The camel lurched forwards a little, and then – like a great monster from the depths of the earth – she let out a roar of victory and clambered up from the wide hole in which she had nearly died. We all fell backwards onto the sand, except for the guide who, wobbly and weak-kneed, led the beast to the safety of the far bank. Recovering ourselves, we returned to fetch the other camel which was calmly chewing in oblivion of our drama, and collected the abandoned baggage which was strewn over the floor of the *oued*. When we joined the guide, he embraced us all, then carefully laid down his blanket under a leafy bush and stretched out to sleep without saying a thing – this we completely understood. An hour later he awoke to have some soup with us and was as exuberant as ever, reliving every second of the adventure and insisting on going back to take a photograph of the 'grave'.

We waited until the most intense heat was over before we set off again, but we were nevertheless weary after the expenditure of so much energy earlier.

The vegetation was now much more abundant, and so were the insects. We were following the course of a *wadi*, and at one point clambered onto a high boulder to see more of the outlying terrain. From here we could see clouds of blue smoke billowing up from behind a screen of palms. The guide became alert, all his senses quickening, having suspected another human presence for some miles. Sliding down off the boulder we approached the shallow hollow from which the smoke was rising, and found ourselves in yet another Tuareg settlement. This time, however, we saw at once that there was a difference: attempts had been made – and on the whole successfully – to cultivate the desert, indicating that these weren't wandering nomads like those we had recently met, but sedentary. We walked past neat oblongs of ground, separated by low hedges of cactus and little irrigation channels in the mud, as we headed in the direction of the fire.

The head of this group was named Fakir. As we approached, he surveyed us coolly from beside the fire where he was sitting, sucking on a weathered pipe. He was shabbily dressed but well-veiled, and commanded great authority; as he rose to his feet his stature and bearing seemed even to impress our guide, who was extending his hand with the civility habitual to all Tuareg. Fakir was alone – at least we couldn't identify any other people through the volumes of smoke – but when he had accomplished all the formalities of greeting us, having welcomed the travellers to his hearth, and having bade us all to sit down, he called out sharply and two boys emerged carrying bundles of green foliage. These they laid next to Fakir, who then asked them to fetch the teapots, and tea things, while he poked the flameless fire in search of a spot hot enough to boil the kettle. It dawned on us that although there was plenty of old dead wood in the region, he burned the green stuff expressly to make smoke – the most effective antidote to all the insects. For the first time in several days we were blissfully free from the minute flies that had plagued us so consistently; the smoke was all-pervading, making our faces smudgy, and our eyes stream with tears, but it was like balm to us! Fakir was as friendly and hospitable as his kinsfolk had been and made the tea with great ceremony. We were joined by his wife and two younger men, one of whom had distinctly negroid features and a very dark skin. The truly 'noble' Tuareg men are known for their light skin-tones, straight hair, fine aquiline noses and, in a very few cases, pale grey or blue eyes. These days, however, owing to greater integration between the varying levels of Tuareg society, these distinguishing features are less common. The skin-tones range from dark to light, the hair varying from person to person; eyes are generally brown, and the shapes of noses and faces can differ enormously. Most of the Tuareg are of slight but tall build, with long legs, narrow shoulders and chests, slender arms and hands, and they move with remarkable grace.

Our brief and unexpected visit to Fakir's homestead was of great interest to us because here we found a living example of the old hierarchical construction of Tuareg society, normally much less obvious these days. The negroid slaves always used to live on a separate level from the vassals, or the nobles, marrying only other slaves except in very unusual circumstances; although they all lived together, each had his own clearly defined role within the society, and the slaves were used for all menial tasks, such as wood-gathering, goat-minding, water-carrying and millet pounding. In such a community, the nobles had the easiest life – especially the women, who were in a position to stay in the shade of the tents, working on leather embroidery, instructing the children, treating and braiding each other's hair, and inventing poetry and songs to sing to the menfolk. The vassal women did the cooking, cleaning, washing and repairing. Nowadays there is considerably less distinction between the women: the noble-women are rarely seen sitting idle, and most of the work that has to be done is distributed evenly amongst them, and is always carried out uncomplainingly, and more or less efficiently.

After an hour at Fakir's settlement, spent enjoying the tea, his company and the freedom from flies, he invited us to go and look around his compound before darkness descended. We were interested to do so, and in particular to identify the source of the continual squeaking sound that we'd been hearing since we came. This turned out to be the clue to the success of the gardens, for, not fifty yards from where we had been sitting, enclosed in a circle of palm trees, was a deep well. In front of the well was an ox, rhythmically pacing to and fro, its harness attached to a pulley. As the ox came towards us, the pulley lifted a soft leather bucket full of water. At a certain point another rope, which was fastened to the base of the bucket, came into effect; when it was pulled taut it upturned the bucket, spilling all the water into a channel made from the hollowed-out trunk of a palm, and thence down into the shallow ditches we had already noticed, flooding a certain plot of ground and then being diverted to the next, the break in the wall of the ditch being dammed up and a further section dismantled so that each patch eventually received its share of watering. Once empty, the bucket was lowered back into the well by the return journey of the ox, and the process was repeated, over and over again, the pulley squeaking throughout like the plaintive call of a bird. Growing in the gardens we saw carrots, onions, turnips and tomatoes, not to mention some bedraggled green plants that we weren't able to identify. Rounding a tight group of palm trees, amongst whose high fronds masses of orange-coloured dates were ripening, we became aware of another's presence, and saw an agile, urchin-like figure stooped over a part of the irrigation ditch, engrossed in a repair. As we spotted him, his eyes also lighted on us, and he at once came forward. We later discovered that he was father to the Negro-featured boy we had met: he was black-skinned and looked like a true Negro in every respect. He was working hard in the gardens, mud up to his knees, while everyone else had finished for the day, except for his wife, who was dredging a section of the channel masked by some leafy shrubs. The implement she was using was like a short broad hoe, typical of the gardening tools used by the Tuareg. She was as black-skinned as her husband and equally disarrayed, with ragged garments loosely pinned about her. It was interesting to see that the man was swathed in the Tuareg *taguelmoust* – but not so surprising since, quite apart from any deeper significance it may have, or any sense of belonging it may produce, the *taguelmoust* is an intensely practical form of headgear: it protects the head from the severe sun during the day, from the cold at night, and from the bite of sand in a storm; it also serves to preserve a tiny area of humidity surrounding the mouth and nostrils so that the dryness of the Saharan air cannot attack them. Nobody quite knows where the *taguelmoust* stems from originally, but it seems reasonable to believe that its use is purely in the interests of comfort. By that token, the women don't wear it because, travelling around less, they have less need of protection from the elements – and their menfolk find them more attractive without it.

The Negro-featured couple we had met, although theoretically freed from the bonds of slavery, were almost servile in their attitude towards Fakir and his wife when we wandered back with them to the fire, now belching clouds of pink-tinged smoke lit by the radiantly setting sun; we thought this attitude created an awkwardness usually absent from Tuareg gatherings. Fakir commanded the old man to show us the apricot grove several hundred yards away: an impressive and memorable sight! Consisting of half a dozen young trees, the grove was a dense and trembling mass of fragrant blossom, completely out of character with the surroundings, and a remarkable achievement under such difficult circumstances. Close by it there was another well, straddled by a pulley construction, but still this time. Under the shade of the apricot trees were some random potato plants, also flowering profusely. Not without justification, the old man and his wife beamed proudly, telling us the whole time that it was nothing but desert before they settled there, which was when their children were babies. We were in for more shocks: concealed amidst the undergrowth was an additional plot of land knee-high in green corn, rippling and undulating in the breeze like an emerald lake in the harsh desert. The woman told us that she and some of the little girls harvested the crop by hand, but that it wouldn't be ripe for several moons.

We were duly impressed by the serenely flourishing community we had stumbled across out of the blue, and were intrigued by the people who lived there, so isolated from the turmoil of twentieth-century living and yet not primitive in the manner of the nomads we had already met. But an even more surprising factor was to come to light. After dark that evening, we ate *cous-cous* with Fakir, his brothers and his sons, and, for the first time in many weeks, we were sitting inside a house. It was one of three or four mud-walled houses with palm-frond thatched roofs, and very low doorways. Inside was a simple room, more or less circular in shape, with two small windows under the overhang of the thatch, curtained by squares of woven palm; the roofs were conical, with a hole in the centre that served as a chimney, as there had to be a fire on which to make tea. Fakir's house was without any furnishings at all, save a little thin blanket on the floor of sand. After the clean air and endless space of out-door life, we felt ill-at-ease and constricted inside: the air seemed stale, and the very individual, sweetish smell of Tuareg leather became overpoweringly dominant in the confined space. We concluded that it must be a blessing during the bleak winter nights when the wind howls and ice forms on the surface of any water left outside, but that in the hot weather the low, sprawling leather tents of the wandering nomads were better ventilated and more suited to the conditions.

We were only able to spend one night at Fakir's village, though he pressed us to stay longer. Our guide was within days of seeing his wife again, and was becoming visibly impatient, not to mention our own schedule which was running almost two weeks late already. Before leaving, Fakir gave us a gift of an old Algerian bank-note, long since obsolete we presumed, which he told us to change in a bank in Algiers and to keep the money as a souvenir of him. Somehow, during the next few days' march we lost it, but at the time thought little of it, believing it to be value-less. We discovered in the capital some weeks later however that it had been worth about seventy-five pounds, and have never taken old notes for granted since!

Fakir also gave us some carefully prepared fly-swatches made from the twigs of an evergreen tree, which he claimed the flies disliked. It is true that we were less troubled by flies while we had those swatches, so perhaps there is some validity in what he said. Fakir had turned out to be quite an eccentric character, and his parting gesture was to unveil his face to reveal a fine grey beard, curly and strong. His head, like most of the Tuareg men, was clean shaven, but he bushed out his beard as much as he could, and insisted we took his picture. This truly amazed us as normally the Tuareg will think twice before unveiling in public, and will never dream of being caught by the camera in the very act.

Having left the settlement behind us, with many a backward glance at the green and blossoming oasis, we continued on the last stretch of our journey. The final few days were more of an ordeal than a pleasure, as the weather was windless and blisteringly hot, and there were masses of insects in the air everywhere. One redeem-ing feature was that as we had eaten most of the food, our baggage was lighter and so the camel could carry everything on her own; at least we hadn't the weight of rucksacks on our backs to hold us back. We were finding the heat quite exhausting, and there was no longer any question of whether we should take a midday rest: none of us felt we had the energy to carry on walking all day. In the afternoon we were back on our feet and walked until nightfall, when we could barely summon the strength to cook dinner, although we always lit a fire for the reasons already mentioned.

One morning that we shall always remember, we were tramping along the edge of a meandering *wadi*, whose course veered from west-east round to east-west and back again, sometimes in the welcome shade of leafy trees and sometimes under the naked sun. All the time we were footsore, we perspired, we felt thirsty and longed for coolness. Rounding yet another bend in the river-bed, our disbelief may be imagined when we found ourselves standing in front of a lake, glittering in the sunlight and crystal clear to its pebbled depths. Without hesitation we followed the guide's example, tore off our clothes and boots, and dived with ecstasy into the clean cold water. We hadn't seen so much water for weeks and weeks, and it had seemed like a mirage when we had first set eyes on it, the answer to an unspoken prayer. The water was pure and indeed cold, only touched by sunshine for an hour or so each day, as it lay under the dark shadow of high rocks. Now it was in the sunshine, and we were bathing in Paradise! We swam, dived, splashed and floated, forgetting our discomfort, our bites and blisters. For over an hour we soaked up the sensation of the soft rain-water on our bodies, emerging refreshed and cleansed. No longer did our scalps feel caked in sand, our skins engrained in it: we all felt re-invigorated and well-equipped to cover the rest of the ground between us and Illizi – our destination.

In spite of the hardships of the last leg of our trek, our final camp was a sad one. Not one of us looked forward to our return to the 'real' world of towns, traffic, shops, houses, televisions and noise, and our guide was plainly as sorry as we were that our experiences together were almost over. We sat around a small fire – kindling being practically non-existent – in the middle of a vast open plain. About us were hundreds of huge, harmless spiders that were attracted to the firelight, scuttling in and out of our legs in a fit of activity. We were only a short walk from Illizi the next day, but we wanted to settle one or two things with the guide that night. We had decided to bequeath our tent to him as he so coveted it, and also to give him a silver watch to be worn on a chain. He had had the loan of this for the trip and had insisted on making us guess the time at least ten times a day, a game which he relished being the only one in the know! He seemed touched and a little overwhelmed by the simple gestures, saying later that they would serve as a very good proof to his friends and relatives of his merits as a guide.

The next morning we walked in silence, hardly even commenting when the towering pylons of the oasis appeared below us. The guide said we were to go straight to the Mayor's office to check in, so we approached the centre of the town directly. Locals looked at us curiously as we strode through the sandy streets, pointing at us and not hiding their amusement. By then we were taking our somewhat bizarre appearance for granted, but at first sight we must have looked oddly weather-beaten and ragged, with deep suntans and very shabby clothes, our boots being the only things that were still completely intact. All our better clothes had been gradually

The gaunt environment of a nomadic encampment. Water is suspended in gerbers *from a tree, to be kept at a cooler temperature by gradual evaporation through the surfaces of the containers. The metal bucket, however, is an unusual possession for the Tuareg*

An unusually ambitious improvised desert 'mosque'. In general, they are cruder and simpler in arrangement, without the dry-stone shelter from which the prayers are recited, and with rows of stones rather than the more elaborate low walls. They are used by the Tuareg nomads, and can be found all over the desert. Not infrequently, an equally simple cemetery can be found in the vicinity of the mosque; a collection of long stones planted on end, in pairs, each pair indicating the head and foot of a separate grave.

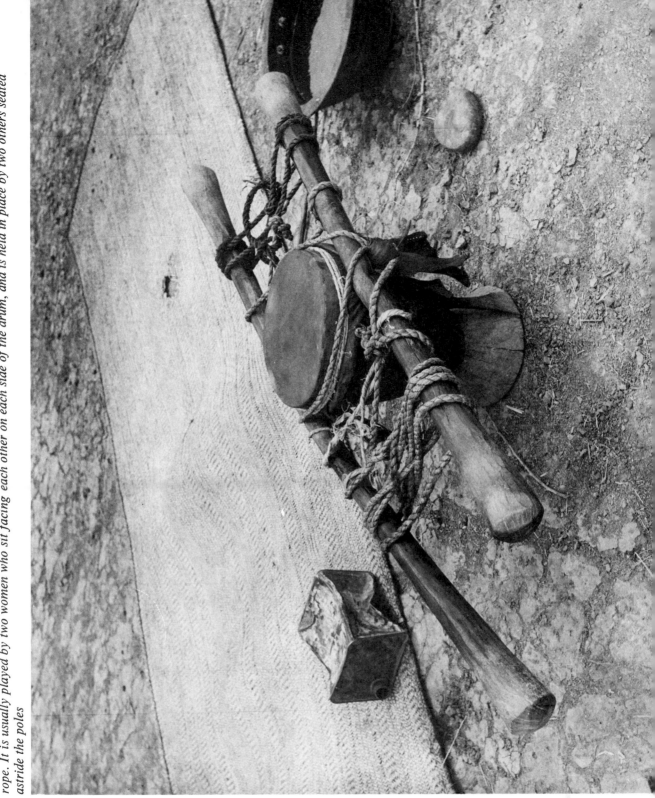

A typical drum of the nomadic Tuareg: a wooden base with skin tautly stretched over it, and two poles strapped on with hand-made rope. It is usually played by two women who sit facing each other on each side of the drum, and is held in place by two others seated astride the poles

A camel man on the Tassili N'Ajjer proudly shows the jaws of his piebald camel. So insensitive is the mouth, that the camel can eat sharp four-inch thorns without damage

donated to nomads, so what was left was tied, pinned or crudely stitched and patched.

The Mayor, a tall dignified Tuareg figure, greeted us royally, and welcomed us into his clean, quiet office. An indolent fan rotated on the ceiling. He gave us coffee and sat behind his large desk before he asked us any questions: we should have been there long ago, he said, and they were beginning to have grave worries on our account – what mishaps had we met? The guide reassured him, however, and his eyes showed us how relieved he was.

The Tuareg who have settled in towns and taken up responsible positions have lost nothing in the magnificence of their dress and carriage, sailing gracefully and unhurriedly through the streets in dazzling white or clear blue cotton robes. Their heads are dressed meticulously in finely pleated *taguelmoust*, and leather purses or silver ornaments swing amidst the folds of their robes as they walk. The Mayor was no exception as he led us solemnly to the 'hotel' of Illizi, acknowledging his friends who strolled up and down in leisurely fashion. The hotel proved to be a sparse and dismal establishment, with rooms more like stables, memorable only for its contaminated beds.

One night there was enough. The next day we were glad to be heading homewards in a rattling station-wagon along a dusty, rutted track, having reluctantly said goodbye to the guide and the two weary camels. We were filled with gratitude to the guide, who had contributed so much to an experience which it might well be impossible to repeat in a few years' time, as the isolation and independence of the Tassili Tuareg is increasingly undermined by both the unyielding terrain and the complete lack of any aid or encouragement from outside their own world.

IV. The Aïr Mountains

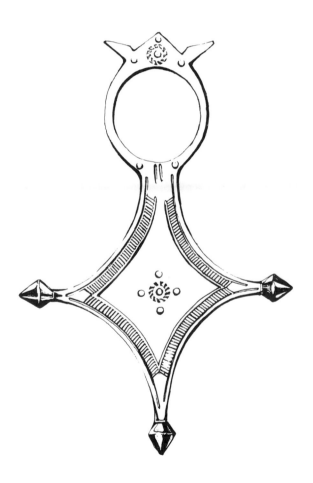

IV. The Aïr Mountains

In the second and third sections of this book we have talked about the Tuareg of the Hoggar and the Tassili N'Ajjer respectively. Now it is the turn of the Tuareg of the Aïr mountains – the most numerous by far. In some ways, they are the least changed by modern pressures, although on this point we are in disagreement with Lloyd Cabot Briggs, who states in his book *Tribes of the Sahara* that the Hoggar Tuareg are the least changed. It would be true to say, however, that many of the new influences on and attitudes of the Hoggar Tuareg have occurred since the publication of that book some thirteen years ago, the most paramount changes being the independence of Algeria, and the prevailing drought of recent years, for nothing is guaranteed to destroy the pastoral nomad's way of life more quickly than lack of pasture.

One of the reasons for the numbers of Tuareg in the Aïr is that, although subjected to the same drought conditions lately, the uplands of the Aïr still have a greater rainfall than many Saharan desert zones. Thus, not only have the indigenous Tuareg been able to continue to live there, but others have gradually had to join them. There are other advantages, too: the Niger Republic is independent, but unlike Algeria no particular majority race holds supreme power. The Hausa (the name ascribed to the people who speak the Hausa language – mainly Negroes) and the Tuareg form the greatest part of the population that averages five people to the square mile; they co-exist, however, with Peulh (or Fulani), Tebu, Djerma, and Arabs, though not many of the latter. An accurate census of the population is impossible because so many of the inhabitants are nomadic and always on the move, and the areas they inhabit are, of course, too remote ever to be found by the census-man. Niger is a very large country, totalling nearly five hundred thousand square miles, but most of the Tuareg are focused on the Aïr Mountains and the Agades area.

Flanked by open desert on one side, and by the foothills of the Aïr on the other, Agades is extremely remote, and grew to be most important as an established market on the ancient caravan trading route linking north Africa with Nigeria, the Sudan and southwards. Once it was a great slave-trading centre, dealing in quantities of slaves every year, as well as being the nucleus of the salt trading organization for the isolated desert salt mines. The mining and trading of salt is still a flourishing industry, and provides employment for many people: the mines are completely unmechanized, and camel caravans are still used to transport the salt from the mines across the hundreds of miles of desert that separate them from the market at Agades. It is only thanks to the deliberate policy of the government that all this has been able to endure, however, as nowadays it would be a viable proposition to have commercial lorries handling all the salt trade transport; the route across the Ténéré could well be marked with posts and the terrain improved for motorized traffic, but the country prefers to maintain its traditional habits of trading, rather than make hundreds of men and their camels redundant and useless. This same attitude was reflected in a conversation we once had with a bright young Lieutenant in the Niger army: in a discussion about the mineral wealth of Niger (or lack of it) he said that he and his fellow-countrymen hoped and prayed that great reserves of oil would never be tapped in Niger; if they were, the country would attract not only a great deal of foreign investment, but also such world interest and interference as to unsettle the local people and destroy their equanimity. 'Take a look at our people', he said. 'They may be poor, but their faces are always smiling; the people in Europe smile less.'

In some instances the salt cargoes are transported as far south as Kano in Nigeria by caravan. Here the camels are given a long rest, are used intermittently for local transport, and then brought northwards again for another season of salt-carrying, bringing goods from Kano to trade in Agades. Near Kano is an entirely Tuareg village where the Tuareg have adopted the Hausa way of life, but they still represent the northern Tuareg people by acting as their agents while they are in the south.

Cattle, sheep, goats, skins and hides form the rest of the trading activity in Agades' sprawling market square. All the other trade is local – glass bracelets, dried herbs, piquant kebabs, crude leather boots, sticks of sugar cane, mountains of ground nuts, and very plain garments, made while-you-wait on old-fashioned treadle sewing machines. All the stalls, which are constructed from wooden frames with woven grass mats flung over them and tied down in haphazard fashion, are neatly arrayed in parallel lines right down the market place. At least a day must be spent in the market alone, absorbing the atmosphere of it all, the beauty of the Hausa women in their flamboyantly coloured prints, the smells of the herbal combinations and the intermingled sounds of the different people and animals. To return there at night is to enter another world: small groups of men and women sit round paraffin lamps and spluttering candles along the outer avenues, selling cigarettes, sweets and cola nuts from trays, or cooking kebabs on wooden skewers over the dim glow of burning

A Targuia wearing silver Agades crosses and other typical jewellery

A young Tuareg tin-miner at Elmiki in the Aïr Mountains

The famous minaret of the great mosque at Agades

Tebu women at Fachi

charcoal. Now the market is still and ghostly – long tunnels of dilapidated stalls casting unearthly shadows under the moon, and here and there a homeless body curled up on a dark corner, snoring gently. The groups of people around the edge either have an expensive-looking transistor radio issuing crackling noises and inter- mittent waves of Arab-music, or they sing their own songs softly, drumming on a bashed tin can and sometimes producing an old penny-whistle or harmonica.

The capital of Niger is Niamey, south-west of Agades and on the banks of the River Niger. Compared to a city like Agades, it is impersonal and modern with its supermarkets and new hotels, humming with traffic and glinting with neon-lit shop signs, but it has, nevertheless a strong African flavour. Its market, selling every imaginable variation of printed cotton, makes the Agades market seem paltry, a mere side show by contrast. But of still greater interest in Niamey is the Zoo- Museum. In its own park, the Zoo has been designed to show animals, birds, reptiles and fish in a habitat as closely corresponding to the natural as possible, and the representation of species is most impressive. The Museum consists of a Natural History section containing well-displayed butterflies, moths, birds' eggs, insects, plants and flowers; a Historical Costume and Jewellery section, with fine examples of local antique dress and ornamentation; and finally – most fascinating of all – replicas of every primitive and nomadic tribal dwelling to be found in the Niger Republic: tents, huts and simple houses, all furnished with the appropriate domestic utensils and equipment of the individual tribes, and all attractively laid out on a grassy slope. Beside the reconstructed dwellings is the Workshop, a constant hive of activity as it is here that all the traditional crafts of the country are practised and kept alive; weaving, copper-beating, wood-carving, pottery, leatherwork, spinning and so on – men, women and children, Fulani, Hausa and Tuareg, all absorbed in their own task. The products of these labours are sold in yet another section of the museum, and the returns are spent on wages, materials and museum up-keep. In view of the rapidity with which so many small tribal customs are dying out, it is heartening to find a community – albeit an artificially created one – whose function is to counteract this tendency, and whose aim is being achieved so successfully. It would be still more heartening to see the same sort of enterprise being applied to many more tourist-orientated centres – although Niamey is hardly a boom-town in that respect – so that tourism could contribute directly to the preservation of all the things from which it benefits so greatly.

Even Agades has what it calls a zoo: opposite the Post Office a fenced-off plot of land, divided into pens, houses half a dozen animals and an ostrich. The ostrich, together with the giraffe, are long-standing inmates who have now been granted the 'freedom of the city', allowed to come and go at will in the streets of Agades all day, returning to the zoo at nightfall to be fed and shut in. The ostrich – a slightly tattered bird – declines to use its privilege very often, but the giraffe is a familiar sight at the petrol pumps, or outside the shops, or just wandering about aimlessly, taken quite for granted.

Because Agades has always contained a cross-section of tribes, including endless divisions in the Tuareg alone, there has been a long history of bloodshed and trouble in the district. Although each tribe had its own chief, there was no over-all power and the chiefs were forever at each other's throats. The situation became so bad that around the beginning of the fifteenth century, even these warring chieftains had to agree on one point: somehow they had to find an independent arbitrator, who would be prepared to step in where required. They decided to approach the Khalif in Istanbul, who, although so far away, then wielded a great deal of power. Over three years passed before the Khalif managed to persuade one of his concubine's sons to take on the job, all his legitimate sons being too pleasure-conscious and comfort-loving to think of leaving home to lead a spartan desert life. In spite of becoming Sultan, he was – according to Tuareg tradition – no better than his mother had been, a mere serf or slave, having inherited none of his father's status. However, this arrangement proved to be an advantage, since it eliminated any possible cause for jealousy amongst the citizens of Agades, who nevertheless had acquired the mediator they sought, which is all his role amounted to. Ever since then it has been an un-written law that the Sultan of Agades must be of low social standing, and this is still observed today.

Despite his lack of nobility, however, he doesn't lack the respect of the people, and this was demonstrated to us once in Elmiki, a tin-mining village in the Aïr mountains. We were staying there when the Sultan paid a courtesy call, staying one night with the Tuareg villagers. The best accommodation was made available, a ritual dinner was prepared and, as darkness fell, a reclining chair was brought out and placed in the open space among the houses, where all the people had assembled to gaze at, or entertain, the visitor. He was young, and very handsome, and solemnly took his seat amidst his entourage while the Tuareg women lined up in the shadows and began to clap and sing. A guttering Kerosene lamp was produced to augment the light of the moon, largely obscured by cloud, and placed on an up-ended petrol drum. As the men started to dance, and the pounding of the feet on the sand stirred up the fine powdery dust, so the clapping of the women grew more animated and the excitement rose in their voices. But the Sultan just sat, impassive and aloof all evening, while a host of anxious henchmen hovered around him.

The administration of Agades is run on French lines, with a Prefecture, and a Mayor's Office. The current 'Prefet' is an imposing young Hausa, striking in the pale clear colours of his finely embroidered *gandoura* against the rich darkness of his skin, a man of great intelligence and charm. His right-hand-man, the 'Sous-Prefet', is a Targui. The first time we visited him at his work we were struck by the dignity with which he handled his affairs – seated gravely behind an expanse of desk piled with papers – while at least ten wrens and finches fluttered prettily about the room, swooping through the open window and even perching on the young Targui's shoulder. We couldn't conceal our amusement, which pleased him and caused him to shed his formal airs. Since then he has shown only the warm and friendly side to his personality, never the busy-bureaucrat.

The desert immediately surrounding Agades is thick with spindly bushes and dry scrub, amongst which small nomadic settlements have been established as well as the ever-shifting groups of low black tents. Eastwards, towards the Ténéré desert, the terrain is hazardous to drive through as the track is deeply rutted by lorries, and the open desert is perforated with gaping holes several feet deep. The surface is caked with a layer of sun-baked mud, over which any vehicle is pitched and tossed like a dinghy in a storm at sea. Delicate grasses, pale and brittle, manage to grow here, disguising the rugged irregularity of the land, and swaying softly, imperceptibly, in the wind. When the sun is low, the grasses seem to be brushed with gold against the darkening sky, in a fairy-tale landscape. However, if mismanaged the fairy-tale environment can soon become treacherous with snares. Some years ago, when we were working in this area for an English tours company who claimed to specialize in safaris, one of the vehicles in the convoy, tired of manoeuvring the ruts in the track, pulled off to the open desert. Within seconds it had overturned and was on its side in a deep pot hole, stuck. The elderly American passengers were badly shaken as they clambered out, the driver saying feebly 'I wasn't watching'. The other vehicles were roped to the upturned one, and the sides of the hole dug away, but even so it took all morning to rectify this mishap. That evening we had camped early and were unloading the vehicles when there was a mighty explosion: flames were leaping up and the decorative grasses shrivelled as a great wave of fire swept through them. We shovelled sand on fast, shifted the closest vehicle, and ran around with the ineffectual fire extinguishers. At last the fire was assuaged, and the passengers stopped screaming. By a miracle no one had been hurt, but damage to the equipment was extensive. 'I wasn't thinking' said the same voice: he had lit a stove not three feet from a five-gallon petrol can, the lid of which was still in his hand. This was one of that company's 'experienced drivers' who, only a few days earlier, had failed to notice that the vehicle ahead had stopped, and had driven straight into its side, wrecking the panels and doors of the two vehicles; 'I wasn't watching' he had said. This man continued his chequered career with the company for some time later, in spite of such incidents.

In this arid and colourless landscape it is a joy to reach a clearing in the thin undergrowth and see several startled gazelle standing motionless, looking directly at us. These are the little Dorcas gazelle, perhaps the most beautiful of the whole deer family, with their enormous dark frightened eyes, fragile bodies and nimble movements. When on the run they move like most deer, with grace and alacrity, in quick controlled leaps, as though a spring had been released inside. They can stop as abruptly as they start, from bounding along they can jerk to a halt, once again taking up a quite immobile position, looking about bewildered and scared. The animal wildlife in the area is limited, but birds are prolific: the largest, if not the most common, is the ostrich, who enjoys this flat country with low vegetation as it enables it to see great distances from beneath its long-fringed eyelashes, and thus be forewarned of any danger. Because of this, it is rare to see them at close quarters from a car. On foot, however, moving slowly and keeping low, we have been able to watch families from within a range of a few yards, as they have no sense of smell or hearing.

For these senses they have to depend on their neighbouring species, who give the alarm in the face of danger. This makes them a sociable breed, choosing to live amongst rather than apart from other creatures. Other birds that are a familiar sight are helmeted guinea fowl, Senegal grouse, bustard, and many smaller species. It is interesting that no in-depth ornithological survey has ever been made of this particular area, probably because of the practical difficulties entailed: the habitat renders a survey of any accuracy at all virtually impossible.

As we get nearer to the edge of the Ténéré desert, the corpses of camels who died en route from the salt mines become more frequent along the wayside, as do Egyptian vultures, either circling ominously in the sky, or gorging themselves on the still fresh flesh of the dead beast. They are so greedy that when given the chance of eating as much as they like, they fill themselves to such an extent that they are unable to fly. This is a curious thing to observe, a vulture running ponderously along the ground, flapping its wings, but incapable of taking off because of the sheer weight of its body. We have seen them stagger to the tops of rocks and hurl themselves desperately into the air – to glide down heavily to the ground. In this area, however, there are no real predators, so they are less vulnerable when in this condition than elsewhere.

'Ténéré' is the Tuareg word for desert, and 'Sahara' the Arabic equivalent. Although contained within the Sahara, the Ténéré has been so named because it is a huge stretch of sand and dunes and little else – no mountains, rocks or river-beds, just infinite sand piled up as far as the eye can see and beyond, for hundreds of miles. It is well-known for its dangers, and many men have perished there because to be lost is to die of thirst within days if not hours. The Niger authorities insist, very wisely, that all who cross this desert should be accompanied by a guide; those who attempt to go it alone invariably end up in disaster.

The Targui guide with whom we always travel across this area reported an incident of as many as eighteen men and one boy perishing at the same time, and not very many years ago. All nineteen of them were in a lorry heading for Libya, via Bilma, on the eastern side of the Tenere, and they were all Libyan Arabs. In Agades they had had to have some work done on the lorry, in the course of which they met a young Arab mechanic who claimed to know the Ténéré and offered to be their guide. They set off thinking this boy would be cheaper than an authorized guide, but the lorry broke down after two days, in the middle of a featureless landscape of sand. They were unable to repair the lorry and began to panic. The young Arab boy had no idea of where they were, but set off walking to look for a well, under pressure from the others. When he didn't return, all the others set off in different directions, running away under the blazing sun – all except one, who realized the inevitable outcome of acting impulsively like this. He waited until nightfall in the shade of the lorry, then, equipping himself with a make-shift shelter and the last of the water, he started to walk. He plotted a vague course by the stars, and walked all night. At daybreak he rigged up his piece of cloth as a patch of shade and rested under it until dusk, when once again he walked. Remarkably, he was able to do this for twenty days, before he collapsed, suffering acutely from dehydration. Unknown to him he was very close to the Asheggour well which is used with relative frequency; he was spotted by Tuareg nomads and taken by camel to Dirkou, an Army post close to Bilma. He stayed there, being cared for by the soldiers, until his strength had been regained, but his mind was still affected and six months passed before he was able to speak a word. It was almost a year since the event before he could at last describe what had happened. As it turned out, the lorry had been found only days after all the men had left. There is logic in the local saying that you should always stay with your vehicle in the desert, even though it can seem like a hopeless solution at the time. None of the other men or their bodies were ever found.

We found this story perfectly credible, after our experience on the Ténéré less than two years ago. By now working for our own company – expressly not a tourist/ safari organization – we had organized an expedition for some hot-air balloonists in the Sahara, which included spending some time on the Ténéré. The terrain here is superb from a ballooning angle, and they in fact broke the official world altitude record for hot-air ballooning. Rising before the sun, the balloonists began to inflate the balloons at first light – in case it proved to be too windy later – so that they could be airborne to watch the sun emerging over the horizon of dunes. As a sport, hot-air ballooning can be both dramatically dangerous and spectacularly beautiful; in competent hands and Saharan conditions there is much more of the latter element, with only fleeting moments of hair-raising incident. Once up, and floating noiselessly over the ocean of dunes, the pilot and his crew could relax and enjoy the sheer magic of the experience, but below they had to be pursued overland in order to be retrieved safely, for should they have dropped out of sight it could have taken hours for them to be found – a situation we were able, by good co-ordination, to avoid. As the balloon rose and fell, so the wind directions changed, wafting the balloon hither and thither in the sky, so that the course of the ground vehicle zig-zagged and swerved all over the desert in pursuit. Our guide, Rhossi, had told us that just before we had left Agades he had been approached by three Italian men in a small saloon car who wanted him to be their Ténéré guide. He had told them that he was just leaving with us, but had given them the name of another Tuareg guide. No one thought any more about this episode, until three weeks later when we returned to Agades. Rhossi happened to make inquiries about the Italians, but no one knew of them. We knew they hadn't arrived in Bilma because we had been staying there: it is a small place and we hadn't seen them. Rhossi then guessed, correctly, what had happened: the Italians, realizing we were crossing, had thought they would save money and time by not hiring a guide and would follow the tracks of our convoy; as there were five Landrovers and a Bedford lorry they must have presumed this would be straight-forward. Not having complied with the regulations about hiring a guide, they were unable to check out officially, so the authorities were unaware of their activities or whereabouts. All would probably have been well if they hadn't started to follow the tracks of the vehicles that had pursued the balloons, leading them round in circles, wasting fuel and time. Enough sand had been blown to obliterate the tracks in places, so the lone vehicle had been driven about in a frenzy, searching for tracks heading to Bilma, until they finally ran out of petrol and so were forced to stop. As soon as he realized what must have happened, Rhossi obtained a vehicle from the Prefecture and set up an official search party. Because of his knowledge of where we had been ballooning, Rhossi was able to take the search party almost straight to the forlorn trio: they were all alive but in a sorry state, having had water up until the day before, but having had almost no food. They were brought in and put into the Agades hospital, where it was pronounced that they could only have endured for very few days more had they not been found. Rhossi was grieved, because nobody gave him a medal!

Breaking down, running out of fuel and getting lost are three of the worst hazards of the Ténéré crossing, but they are also more or less avoidable, given adequate forethought and a good guide. The guide's function is not only to find the way but also to watch the texture and colour of the sand all the time, which tells him where to drive and where to avoid. To set off with no prior knowledge or experience could mean being bogged in the sand every few hundred yards, which entails having to stop, get out, dig out the sand from around the wheels, lay down the sand ladders or sand mats (made of lengths of heavy-duty canvas reinforced with ribs of metal threaded through at regular intervals), and push for dear life, all under the burning glare of the sun. Even when the wheels are freed and the vehicle is moving again, it generally has to be driven some distance in order to find a safe place to stop, while the people who pushed are trailing along in its wake, feet dragging in the hot soft sand, and sand blowing into red-rimmed eyes. It is not impossible, but it is rare to cross the Ténéré with a heavily laden vehicle and not get sand-bogged once. It is easier for four-wheel drive vehicles, but they are not an absolute necessity. One European in Agades, who has lived there most of his adult life, crosses the most treacherous parts of the Ténéré regularly in his Peugeot saloon. He doesn't get stuck, and he does the journey to Bilma and back in half the time it takes a heavy vehicle. When we first knew him he was making a living as manager of the government-owned Agades hotel, which he did well. Now he has turned his lush green garden, about seven miles from the town of Agades and full of citrus fruit trees, exotic flowers and decorative birds, into a camping ground. He has built a bar, a dance floor, a cooking area and is planning a restaurant, but the greatest attraction of all is the irrigation reservoir which does dual service as a swimming pool. Early on in our acquaintance with him the garden was a haven of peace and solitude, with only the sounds of the birds and the cicadas, and the slow gurgle of water flowing through the gardens to interrupt the silence. Now cars come and go, transistors blare, pressure-cookers hiss over burners that roar, and there is a constant cry and babble of voices: indistinguishable from a camp site anywhere else in the world, and increasingly in demand.

Beyond the hidden, tree-encircled garden is the open vegetable garden in which two Tuareg brothers work all day. They are Idrissa and Aburachman, and they embody all the physical characteristics of their people. When working they wear only the traditional black widely pleated trousers, and a black cotton *taguelmoust* around their heads. They are both tall and thin, sinewy-limbed and strong, with narrow shoulders, chests and hips, and muscular backs. When the *taguelmoust* slips down, it reveals their straight, even features and close-cropped black hair. During the day's work they wear no sandals, but they are never without their stone-arm-bands, originally worn to protect their arms in battle, or the many leather wallets suspended from their necks. Although they have clung rigidly to this traditional appearance, they have surrendered perhaps the most important Tuareg tradition of all – their dignity and reserve. It has been replaced by an embarrassing, fawning servility towards Europeans, which has probably been knocked into them by the French colonialists, and which they have found necessary to sustain in order to keep their jobs as gardeners in the employ of a European. In their own homes there is not a trace of this obsequious behaviour; when they put on the rest of their clothes at the end of the day – a white shirt under the white cotton overdress and the flat leather sandals – and re-arrange the *taguelmoust*, they assume their true personalities again, becoming authoritative and bold. Their wives live in very much the same way as the pastoral Tuareg nomads in the mountains, fetching water every day from the garden, pounding their own millet, grinding their own corn and rearing livestock. Although they are based near Agades, they don't necessarily go there very often, forming a largely self-sufficient little community. They do not use the hospital or medical treatment that is available, unless they regard it as a matter of life or death. Customarily, the women deliver their own babies either quite alone, or with a female relative or a close friend to help by rubbing the mother's body with fat or oil; a minimum of fuss is made of all such matters, and ordinary life is picked up exactly where it was dropped just before the birth. Surprisingly few babies die at birth, yet they are treated in an off-hand manner from the start, wrapped in an old rag and put in the shade, or strapped astride the mother's back in a strip of cloth tied over her chest. Breast-feeding goes on for as long as possible, the mother feeding as many of her children as she can without depriving the newly born baby.

It was Idrissa's wife who first showed us how to bake bread in the sand as the Tuareg do. She had been grinding corn all morning so that she would have enough flour for the loaf. Once it was mixed into a dough, well-kneaded, and patted into a large, round, flat shape, it was dusted with the remains of the dry flour and put on one side. The fire, which had been burning for an hour or so, then became the sole object of her attention: with a short stick she raked the embers to one side, and made a flat space in the clean hot sand underneath. The dough was then gently lowered into the space and quickly covered over with hot sand, and the glowing embers were replaced on top. She left it for twenty minutes – although she had no idea how long it was, saying simply that you had to wait for the right length of time to pass – and then unearthed the loaf, turned it over and carefully covered it again with the very hot sand and embers. A further passage of time – of exactly twenty minutes – and the loaf was baked. The dry flour had effectively prevented any sand or grit from penetrating the dough, but to be doubly sure, the Tuareg always wash the new loaf in water, reducing the mouth-wateringly crusty loaf to a rubbery pulp, which they always eat with relish.

Several hundred miles to the east of Agades, and slightly to the north, on the far side of the Ténéré desert, lies Bilma, one of the most remote oases in the whole world. It is in such an extraordinarily isolated situation, surrounded as it is by the desert of rolling dunes, and a perilous cliff-face, that it is used as a natural prison; mile after mile of trackless and uninhabited terrain provide an effective barrier between prison inmates and the outside world, so that most of the limited number of prisoners there are able to lead a relatively normal life, and sometimes even decide to settle there on being 'released'.

It has been a flourishing salt-mining community for centuries, never developing noticeably in output of salt, or in the techniques of mining it. In the red-brown earth of the desert around Bilma, the salt gives the ground a frosty, crystal-like sheen. In order to extract the salt, wide oblong pits have been dug and filled with water into which the salty earth is scattered. Little by little the salt separates from the earth and rises to the surface, while the earth sinks to the bottom. There is an extensive area of these pits, the water ranging from thick and brackish to nearly clear, each pit representing a different stage of the process, and each with a crust of salt on the surface. As fast as the crust of salt forms it has to be broken in order to allow the water to evaporate, since it is only through the process of evaporation that the salt particles can gather on the surface. It is not uncommon to see the salt-miners urinating on the crusty surface to break it up, but the resulting salt is only used for animal consumption. Once the maximum has been extracted, the salt is scooped out onto the side of the pit and pressed into a mould, made from a hollowed palm trunk measuring about three feet in height; it stands in the mould for several days, by which time it is hard enough for the mould to be removed and for the columns of salt to be packed onto the backs of the waiting camels.

Two categories of salt are mined at Bilma, the latter being the less pure and destined for animals. The purer form, whiter and cleaner than the other, is not moulded into columns but into round cakes of about ten inches in diameter. These are formed in the base of a gourd, or – more commonly these days – in an enamel bowl, and upturned to dry out in the sun, on the 'sand-pie' principle. They are then carefully packed one on top of the other, as they sell for slightly more than the cruder salt on the market. Before being loaded both types are wrapped in straw-matting and tied around with rope. Two Tuareg are needed for the loading of each camel, which is both a lengthy and exasperating task. The camel is loaded in kneeling position, so that it is at least more manageable at that point than a mule or a horse, for instance. A baggage saddle is strapped around its girth, which acts as a platform on which to secure the salt loads, and as a protection for the camel's flesh, since the camel is very susceptible to sores; once a sore is started due to pressure or rubbing from the load, it can take a long time to heal and not surprisingly makes the camel even more reluctant to be loaded. When the load has been prepared, the two men each take a bundle – weighing up to two hundred pounds – and lean them against each side of the camel simultaneously, taking the weight against their bodies while they attach them together at the top with two sticks threaded through the loops of rope around the loads. When they stand back the camel takes the full weight and at once starts to complain, baring its great yellow teeth and bellowing heartily. The greatest effort is required when it has to stand up; first it leans back and rises onto its fore-knees, then it lurches forward and straightens its back legs, finally staggering off its knees onto its feet and levelling the load. Not infrequently it sheds its load in the act of standing up; if not, the chances are that it will bump into the load of another camel, dislodging the carefully balanced burden, whereupon of course the men have to start all over again. It isn't until the camel is up and walking about that the men can judge how secure the load is and how well the weight is distributed.

In the early days of the Bilma salt caravans, vast numbers of camels used to be involved; on one historic occasion thirty thousand camels were recorded as participating in one caravan. Even now a major caravan can number as many as five thousand, but the largest one we have seen consisted of about one thousand two hundred, and we were rather impressed with that! Of course the caravans of really tremendous size were a great temptation to raiders such as the Tuareg of old, but with French administration, and the introduction of the Camel Corps – a desert patrol unit who travelled solely by camel – a close watch and a tight guard was maintained over the caravans as they progressed, which more or less put an end to the activities of the desert highwaymen.

The camels in a caravan may belong to many different owners, to just one, or to several. Very often the owners do not accompany their camels, hiring cheap labour to tend the animals and putting one trusted man in charge. Each camel is branded with a particular sign to indicate ownership, and if by any chance a camel should die of exhaustion during the long march or should have to be killed for any reason, such as breaking a leg, the hired hand must always cut out the branded sign to take back to the owner as a proof that he had not sold the camel to anyone en route. In the past it was almost exclusively Tuareg who operated the caravans, but now it is not unusual to see some Hausa intermingled with them; the Peulh are never involved as they are brought up with cattle and have no affinity whatsoever with camels; the Tebu are hardly ever involved as they are not generally trusted, but occasionally Djerma men are hired for the work.

Once we came upon a caravan at rest on the Ténéré. Rhossi grew very excited because it was his caravan, comprised of only his camels – about fifty of them, which represents quite a fortune. Naturally enough, he had been anxious about the welfare of his entire capital in the hands of other men, and so was delighted that we should meet. We were heading for Bilma, while they were returning to Agades, with only three days' marching to go. As we neared the patch of desert in which they had chosen to settle down for the night, we saw signs of men stirring, though all the camels were still in their kneeling, sleeping position. Plumes of smoke were rising in perpendicular columns as early tea was brewed: it was half past six and the sun had only been showing for a matter of minutes. The state of the encampment seemed at first glance to be one of complete disorder, with bundles, bits of rope, and sprays of hay littered over quite a large area of sand, but when we had had time to observe the activity we could appreciate that there was a certain logic in the chaos. The hay had been shared out amongst all the animals once they had been unloaded and had settled down: there was not a single blade of pasture in the area, so the camels had been hobbled in kneeling position, by binding a cord around one of their bent knees, to encourage them to rest rather than roam. The bundles, mainly of salt but some sacks of dates, were deposited in pairs in the vicinity of the camel that had carried them, with the pack saddle, rope and sticks strewn about in the same region. The men had few personal belongings other than what they stood up in: there were communal pots for the dinner, and kettles which were always fixed to the camel's load last of all, to clank and bang rhythmically against each other all day long. Twigs, dried grasses and broken branches were also scattered about, to be left deliberately for a subsequent caravan that might be short of fuel: there was no risk of anyone profiting undeservingly from a gesture of this sort, for the code of the caravan is a strict one, and each member does-as-he-would-be-done-by at all times.

The men and their charges were quiet, all still blurred with such a brief sleep and enjoying the peaceful sunrise before the hard pace of the day's march. They had walked far into the cool of night the previous evening, not stopping to sleep until long after midnight. This was quite a customary pattern, and they would now spend several hours packing up and loading before hoping to start walking again. Once they had started, they would not stop at all until half-way through the night, as it was unfair to kneel the camels unnecessarily with such loads, or to break the rhythm of the march for a brief stop: four hours was the minimum period they would halt for, so that at least the animals could rest.

Rhossi was met by the head man as we wandered over, and seemed pleased with the way in which he found everything. The man he spoke to was his cousin, but physically they bore no resemblance to each other at all, the cousin having all the characteristics of a true Targui, while Rhossi is a true exception: he is always pleading poverty, but he must be the fattest and best-fed Tuareg alive, as well as one of the most jovial and most respected. Round-faced, plump-featured and fair-skinned, it would be difficult to place him if encountered out of context. He is never without the *taguelmoust* around his head, but on the occasions when he takes it down to re-arrange it, he shows off his smoothly shaved scalp with pride. In his middle thirties only, he has an unusually sound knowledge of the Ténéré, which he learnt from his youth spent in the Camel Corps, when for months at a time they would simply patrol the desert areas to ensure that all was well. He speaks very good French, also learnt with the Camel Corps, as well as all the local tongues, and has an endless fund of desert adventure stories, now becoming rivalled by his Funny Tourist stories, with which he amuses his family for hours into the night. We all had glasses of tea with the caravan men, while they told us of the trouble at Fachi, the oasis they had called at for water after leaving Bilma – the only oasis between Bilma and Agades and even then considerably out of the way. Evidently the authorities had had to be called in because there had been a series of complaints about the date crops being stolen from the palm trees at night, and the local inhabitants had been unable to catch the culprits or even find their footprints. The Sous-Prefet at Bilma had been contacted, who had sent some Tuareg over with arms, but in the end it turned out that the Tebu had organized their children to go to the palm groves on camels, stand on the camels' backs and reach up to the dates, deftly cut them down and ride off with them. They had been caught and the parents identified, but – as the Tuareg put it – it was a matter that would have to be settled between themselves, and the true story probably started long before this incident; there was no speculation or moralizing. The Tuareg have a proverb which says 'Reasoning is the shackle of the Coward'.

Rhossi was well satisfied with the state of his caravan, and so when the men began the business of loading we thought it best to leave. The length of time involved in the double-crossing of the Ténéré is about three weeks, from leaving Agades to returning there, and all the fodder for the camels has to be taken along for both outward and return journeys as there is no pasture on the way, and none at Bilma either. Camels can only endure for long periods without water if the pasture is exceptional, when they can last for several weeks, but when the pasture is dry – as it is in the Ténéré – they have also to be watered every few days. For a while before a caravan starts out the camels are discouraged from drinking, so that when confronted with water just before the departure, their thirst is so great that they drink until their bellies are nearly bursting, and then they have enough water stored to keep them going for longer. In spite of its reputation as a hardy animal, the camel requires a great deal of attention if it is to live a long time: its pasture must be of the right consistency, for too rich a diet can cause as much disease as too impoverished a diet can; it is prone to sores which, unless treated early, become rapidly septic and gangrenous, infecting its bones and poisoning its system, and several fatal sicknesses can occur if the animal is overworked or under-nourished. The Tuareg have devised remedies for all the ailments, however, which include blood-letting, rubbing with powdered donkey droppings, mixtures of oil and ashes (for treating mange), lotions made from female camel urine, concotions of onion, tobacco leaf and mustard-like seeds mixed with water, and tobacco snuff in the eyes. All these cures are instantly effective if administered in time: hard to believe, but true! The two commonest types of Tuareg camel are the Tibesti and the Ghati, the latter being the one that does most of the work. This is a well-built, shorter and tougher breed than the Tibesti, which is normally used for riding, with its longer legs and lighter build. The Tibesti camels are sometimes brown, sometimes piebald and sometimes pure white, the white ones being very highly prized and treated almost with reverence. A reasonable camel now costs in the region of eighty pounds, but a really good one, such as a cow-camel that has calved once, can be considerably higher. The females are less worked in general than the males, as they are weaker in constitution and build, and have less stamina.

On one occasion when we were entering Niger at its border with Algeria, we were left in the company of a family of Tuareg nomads while our passports were inspected – an unaccountably lengthy procedure. The nomads also had to 'show papers', each adult being equipped with an Identity Card, a highly valued possession, produced with pride at the least provocation because of its portrait photograph. The nomads had very few goods and chattels: rolls of blanket, sacks of food, some pots and pans, all loaded onto two camels. On a third camel, however, was an elaborate cage-like construction made from stripped branches in the shape of a great hood, built over the ordinary Tuareg saddle. This was intended as a protection against the sun for long journeys and had enough room for at least two women with young children to sit across; a strange sight and one we have never seen again. The Tuareg riding saddle is not used at all on the caravan trail as, if the men aren't walking beside the camels, they simply sit on top of the load. But for the usual journeys undertaken by the pastoral nomad, a curious design of saddle is used with a cross-shaped support at the front of the seat, and a simple back-rest behind. The saddle is made of wood, bound with leather, and the cross-shape is nearly always ornately coloured and decorated. It is a practical design as it serves both to prevent the rider from slipping forwards onto the camel's neck, and as a handle to grip when the camel moves faster. This saddle is a distinctive feature of the Tuareg culture, and is unlike any other.

The Tebu people, whom we heard mentioned in connection with the trouble at Fachi, are originally from the Tibesti mountains in Chad, but have now spread farther afield and tend to be found in small numbers throughout the oases of Niger. An early contact we had with them was an unusual one: we came across two men sitting beside the dirt-road early one morning in the region of In-Gitane, apparently eating their breakfast. They had gleaming dark brown skins, and were short in stature. Both were wearing wide-brimmed straw hats and were sitting each side of a big round gourd from which they were eating. As we walked over, they stood up to greet us, invited us to sit down and offered us a spoonful of their breakfast, which looked like porridge. Not wishing to be offensive, we both drank a large spoonful, and tasted a curious combination of flavours: it was like millet, mixed with sour milk and sugar, but it had a generous portion of violently hot chili powder added to it, giving an overpowering and burning aftertaste, the effect of which we were unable to disguise. The two men showed wild surprise, then wild amusement, pressing us to take some more. We asked them what they were doing out here in the stark open desert, and they told us: practising archery. Beside them lay two bows and a dozen long pointed arrows, but one of the bows was broken, which is why they had stopped for breakfast. We helped them to fix the broken bow and then asked them to show off their skill. One of them leapt up eagerly, ran a distance of twenty feet at the most, propped his wide hat against a stick in the sand to serve as a target, and sauntered back to show us how it was done. He took up an obscure pose, and aimed very carefully, shutting one eye, screwing up his features and pulling the bow back as far as he could. With a 'ping' and a 'whoosh' the arrow flew through the air – not to the centre of the hat; not even in the direction of the hat – but sailed through the air ten feet away from the deliberate target! His friend was doubled up with laughter, and after his first look of astonished disbelief, he too laughed. They laughed like hyenas – until the second one made his attempt. Very seriously he went through the same motions, and missed by about the same margin. More hysterical mirth! We finally left them – both rolling in the sand like two circus clowns, their laughter ringing in the silent desert air.

The areas around Fachi and Bilma and northwards were at one time more or less controlled by the Tebu, but towards the end of the seventeenth century a battle took place between them and the Tuareg, out of which the Tuareg emerged victorious. There are still Tebu living in these oases, but they are in the minority, with a few exceptions. Bilma is mainly Hausa and Tuareg, as are Fachi and Seguedine; Dirkou is an army encampment which is now semi-derelict, but still further north at Chirfa and Djado, the population – although very low – is almost exclusively Tebu. Djado is a picturesque ruin of a town; its dilapidations cling bravely to the mountain top, but when silhouetted against the flaming sky of evening it is a forbidding abandoned city. The mountain stands in a thick bed of palms that shelter soft green grass from the seering sun. From amidst the high ruins a long view of the desert all around is afforded, the sand lilac-pink on the horizon, whiter as it gets nearer, turning to the lush, vivid green of the oasis with pools of water glimmering beneath the trees. Also beneath the trees are thousands of mosquitoes and their larvae, malarial mosquitoes that destroy human life; they are now the sole inhabitants of the town, save the scattering of Tebu nomads around the mountain who have developed natural immunity. The mosquitoes thrived on the blood of the people of Djado, causing such disease and tragedy that the survivors packed up and left – their numbers having already been gravely depleted by wars.

Chirfa – five miles from Djado – is also populated by Tebu nomads only, who scratch a living in the forgotten village with their chickens and goats. Facing the empty desert there is a ruined and long-deserted Foreign Legion fort, now half-submerged in sand, whose battlements still echo with the cry of Legionnaires. The Tebu women with their strong bone-structure and well-proportioned features can be strikingly handsome; some wear the silver ring through one nostril, and some the very distinctive hairstyle of a lump of matted hair directly over the forehead, but the dress, of necessity, is very simple.

Not far from Djado and Chirfa is a moon-like landscape of rocks, which we have stopped several times to explore when on the route northwards from Bilma. The fingers of rock interlace along the edge of a great flat plain fringed on all sides with mountains and sand dunes. There are smooth, towering outcrops, and low irregular platforms with craggy surfaces. Pale sand, clean and smooth, runs between them, climbing up some surfaces in a curving drift. There are long valleys like wide boulevards, flanked with boulders and filled with silence, then a tumbling river-bed strewn with stones and fallen rock with weather-worn cliffs on either side. There are brief tunnels under some of the rocks, empty and dark, and there are pebbly clearings, enclosed, hidden even from the wind. The terrain rolls on like this for miles. The last time we were there happened to be the night of the full moon. We had arrived purposefully in the morning and chose an idyllic place to make our camp, in a wide shallow cave deep in sand on a ledge facing west, backed by the vast shoulder of the mountain behind. During the day we walked for miles, starting out with one simple objective: to see as much as we could of this extraordinary landscape. Following the course of a *wadi*, however, we spotted a long ledge in the face of a cliff which seemed interesting. Clambering up on to it we immediately found a cave whose walls were painted with animals, though the shapes were only faintly visible. We were excited to discover that, as we had thought, the area must at one time have been inhabited by prehistoric man, and at once began a frenetic search of the area for more signs. Within the space of half an hour, we had found a distinct painting of a giraffe, simple in line and small in scale, finely executed and clearly coloured. Given these incentives we scoured the rock walls all around, finding good and less good examples – one of the best being an engraving of an elephant on a fallen boulder. Again the scale was small – it measured less than twenty inches – which made us even happier to have come across it. Regardless of whether others have been before, the thrill of finding something independently is still a great joy, and must be one of the reasons we keep returning to the Sahara. In this instance we cannot be sure whether others have or have not seen the prehistoric rock art, but since the whole area is known to contain some evidence of prehistoric habitation, it is not unlikely that they have.

Once we had made a cursory exploration of the outlying rock surfaces, we began to search the ground. Where there was an abundance of potsherds we started to dig the top level away, carefully examining each scoop of sand. In one area only were we particularly successful, finding first a crude axehead, then a section of a beautifully shaped stone bracelet, perfectly smooth, in hard grey stone. Never having found any stone jewellery before, we were now content to call off the hunt; and in any case the afternoon light was beginning to mellow and we still had a walk of several miles back to the camp. On our return we were interested to cross the path of a desert fox whose footprints were clearly defined in the sand. Although we saw only one or two beetles and a crow, the footprint-count was high in this area, including *djebboas* (the playful sand-coloured mice that hop), spiders, lizards, snakes and a variety of small birds, but obviously they preferred to come out when they had the place to themselves and resented our intrusion.

We arrived back at the cave just before the sun vanished over the low mountain backdrop, and so were able to sit and watch the universe turn from every glorious shade of red to bands of luminous purple and green – and finally to black. While we prepared food, the full moon was rising – an enormous disc forging its passage through the tide of stars, its intensity brightening to dim theirs. Equipped only with a good pair of binoculars, hour upon hour may be spent staring at the face of the full moon; in an atmosphere of this clarity, so much detail jumps into focus, and that night we fell asleep engrossed in the moon, binoculars resting on our faces till dawn.

The next day we had to leave the 'Col des Chandeliers' – as the area is called – early in the morning, but we always look forward to returning there, as it is one of the few places we know that cannot or will not have changed too drastically in the interim. A striking contrast to this is the oasis of Fachi, an area that was literally changed overnight. Remote and inaccessible as it is, with no tracks to or from it, but simply pillows of dunes in every direction, it has never been a popular port of call for the average traveller. It was rare for anyone to go there unless they had to, for the dunes are a strong deterrent to even the most ardent desert-lover. As an indication of how foolhardy it is not to respect the dangers the dunes represent, it is worth mentioning the tourist safari company who thought they could drive to Fachi without a guide, having done the route so often. Inevitably, there were problems: they became lost, and this proved fatal for one member of the party. Nine others were hospitalized but luckily survived. Less than a decade ago, when the Fachi people were still barely familiar with the features of a European face, a film unit arrived in Fachi to make a film. Money, apparently, was no object, and it proved an *entrée* to everywhere in Fachi. Given enough lavish presents, the children behaved as required, and could even be directed. The unit stayed only a few days, but its impact has stayed to this day. As this was their first real contact with Europeans, the Fachi people accepted them as the norm, and now use them as the yardstick in their minds by which to measure all European visitors. Therefore, unless the visitor is laden with gifts, with money to place in each and every outstretched palm, he must expect to be jeered at, spat at, and have a stream of unwarranted abuse thrown at him. But the fault does not lie solely in the Fachi people. The money of a flourishing film company is so readily used as the facile means to an immediate end, but it can also do a lasting disservice to the world, unless some time and thought is given to achieving the same result in a less damaging way.

After a period of time on the Ténéré, it is always with a pang of regret that we find ourselves eventually heading back to Agades, or alternatively up through the northern Ténéré towards Djanet and the Tassili N'Ajjer. The scenery of the northern Ténéré, once beyond the area of the Col des Chandeliers, must be some of the most monotonous in the world – gravelly expanses of boring, unrelieved flatness, lacking in any feature more interesting than a marker post. At least the western Ténéré has the undeniable beauty of its dune formations, over which it is a wondrous experience to wander, as well as the interest of all the caravans that pass that way. Even the caravans are not infallible, however, on the question of finding their way over the Ténéré, as we discovered once when returning from a crossing of the desert with Rhossi. The most vital landmark on the Ténéré is a straggly tree, 'L'Arbre du Ténéré', because it is the only one for miles and miles and marks the location of a well. Finding that well means the difference between life and death for the Agades-bound caravans, for by the time they reach that point the camels need watering again, and they are still at least three days' walk from Agades at an average pace. As an addax once fell down the well and drowned, the water is too contaminated for humans to drink. The patch of desert around the well is littered with the bleached bones of camels who were left at the well to die. The latest victims attract vultures for a few days, then just beetles and ticks: the sand swarms with aggressive, biting insects. The tree also marks the change of scene between the slightly varying landscape of some green vegetation – which appears overnight after the most fleeting shower of rain – scrub, hills and trees towards Agades, and the rolling rising and falling dunes of the Ténéré desert. In the former there are people, livestock and tracks, while in the latter there are only the dunes. Even the plucky little gazelle gives up in the face of so much sand, and stays on the edge (where it must exist in some numbers, judging from the quantity that an Army Lieutenant and two soldiers can shoot in a few hours, and which were shown to us proudly, once they had been skinned and gutted and hung from the Tree in neat rows to dry out, at which we couldn't disguise our real dismay).

Driving out into the dunes, the tree was some ten miles behind us when Rhossi saw a black speck in the distance. He told us to head straight for it. It was a man and he was running, running in despair at the thought of our passing by without seeing him. He was from a caravan which had missed the tree. When they first realized this they had turned round, confident they could still find it. Again they must have passed it, because now they were quite lost and they had not a drop of water left. He was understandably agitated and distraught. We gave him a drink of water and then drove him back to his caravan, giving them all the water we could spare, while Rhossi explained to them exactly how to locate the tree. We left them, and heard later that they had managed to find it the third time – though Rhossi said they had been incredibly lucky to have been found, as they would otherwise almost certainly have perished. Another time we met the remains of a caravan that had been less lucky: first we found a dog sitting directly in our path; as we approached, it stood up but was unable to bear its own weight and sat down again. Before we even stopped we could tell it was nearly dead – a pathetically cadaverous corpse that was still somehow alive. Rather than letting it suffer on, we knew we had to kill it, but this was by no means an easy job. A swift blow between the eyes, and it keeled over, almost gratefully – but anticipating it had made it difficult. Then, not very much further on, we spotted a camel wandering alone. It was in an even worse condition than the dog, its bones actually protruding through its flesh in places, with the droppings of a crow on its back, where the bird had perched to peck at the open sores, doing awful damage with its vicious beak. Rhossi said the only way to prevent this from happening was to tie the wings of a dead crow onto the camel's back, when for some reason no live crow will go near it. This time he agreed to kill the poor beast and he did it quickly and effectively, not forgetting to cut out the patch of skin with the brand mark on it so that he could locate the owner back at Agades and explain what had happened. Our hearts sank when yet another aimlessly wandering camel came into view, and Rhossi told us not to stop. However, we had to stop to see if we could do anything, and we were glad because this time it seemed that it might well survive, given a basin or two of water. We gave it five gallons and watched its belly swell slightly as it sucked it all up thirstily. Apparently it would then rest until nightfall, when it would walk all night towards Agades. In two nights it would be back, said Rhossi, and it would certainly find its way as camels have an extra-ordinary sense of direction. Once again he proved to be perfectly correct.

A Targui of the Aïr Mountains outside his tent at Kourboubou

Tuareg women and children at Kourboubou

We felt that to come across three animals within so short a distance of each other was a sign that there would be more, but on this Rhossi was very firm: of course there would be more, and probably some men amongst them, but it was much too risky for us to start looking for them, especially since we were now five gallons lighter and couldn't spare any more water, let alone fuel. We had to accept this as law, but it is always difficult to appreciate how much more dearly we value life than the Tuareg do, their way of life demanding a more fatalistic, or realistic, attitude to death.

The present Saharan drought perhaps provides the ultimate example of the strength of their fatalism even in the face of horrifically adverse conditions. The drought has now reached such grave proportions as to attract world attention at last, but it has been affecting every aspect of the nomad's life for the past seven years. Even if the nomad himself can survive, his way of life cannot. His beasts fall visibly by the way-side, and he is more dependent on his beasts than on any other single factor: for meat, milk, and transport; for hair to weave and leather to sew.

After enduring seven years of increasing aridity and destitution, it is possible that the countries affected by the drought have asked for outside help too late. Their national pride perhaps prevented them from enlisting such aid in time, and now that it is forthcoming, how helpful is it? During a recent expedition which we mounted in the Mauretanian desert, we were to witness the misguided nature of some of the aid that is being poured in. We saw lorry-loads of blankets, crates and crates of dried milk, but we felt that, given a minimum of first-hand experience and some imagination, these efforts could well have been spread over so much more worthwhile areas than is the present case, to relieve the poverty and suffering of whole nations.

As so often happens in the African nations, the United States are making massive donations of goods; at the time of writing, there are no less than 60,000 tons of food and other supplies in storage on the coast of Senegal. But as road communications between Senegal and Mali no longer exist, and those between Senegal and Mauretania are not good, facilities for transporting all the goods into the interior are minimal. The United States Air Force has supplied three aircraft, the Niger Rose, the Bamako Belle and the African Queen, specifically to fly the supplies into the drought-stricken regions. The task they have undertaken is gigantic. The death rate amongst the domestic animals alone is now well into five figures, and fast increasing every day. The human toll is no less tragic: many are dying, many more are being forced to forsake the open desert for the cramped suburbs of the towns.

Nearing Agades, the very individual minaret of the Great Mosque can eventually be seen thrusting upwards through the surrounding savannah, dominating the town and the desert for many miles around. This minaret is unique architecturally, having been built originally in 1844 and destroyed in 1847 by the rainy weather which washed away its hard clay surface, causing it to crumble to the ground. The Sultan of the day had it rebuilt straight away, ordering that it should have cross beams jutting out on the exterior like the spines on a hedgehog, to facilitate maintenance. Since then it has been regularly patched up after any rain, and has suffered no more damage.

At first it was used as a true minaret, to the top of which a *Muezzin* climbed daily, then as a watch tower, for obvious reasons, but now it serves no other purpose than acting as a landmark and the focal point of Agades.

Although Rhossi has a house in Agades, he lives in a village some twenty miles outside, called Kourboubou, which we had visited one day for tea. Here we met his family, with the exception of his father who was then the head of the village, and too old to leave his tent – in fact Rhossi's elder brother made most of the decisions relating to the community in practice. During the summer when the pasture dries up, the village is abandoned and the inhabitants move to another village, called Abelama, far on the other side of Agades, as we learnt to our cost. We had said on one occasion that we could collect Rhossi from Abelama prior to a Ténéré crossing. Before leaving Agades to fetch him, we asked his cousin who was accompanying us, how far it was, so that we would know how much fuel we would need – forgetting momentarily that if a Targui is asked a question to which he doesn't know the answer, he considers it rude to be so dull as to say 'I don't know', and invents an answer that is likely to please. The cousin said brightly 'Ten kilometres there and back'. Reassured we set off, knowing we had more than enough fuel. When the fuel gauge showed that half of it had been used up we asked how much further it was. 'One kilometre' – spoken with admirable conviction! By the time we ran out of fuel we had been driving for two hours and still had seen no signs of Abelama, though we had seen many other interesting things. These included a family of ostrich running along the track before us, the two parent birds at each side and three young ones in the middle. With its long stride and ill-proportioned body, the ostrich makes a curious spectacle when running at full stretch, but its speed – even when young – demonstrates aptly why its wings, through the gradual process of evolution, became obsolete; no creature that can run at such a rate needs also to be able to fly.

When the Landrover jolted finally to a halt, we remembered a spare can of petrol that we had by chance in the back. It didn't contain much but it turned out to be enough to get us at least as far as Abelama, where Rhossi was sitting in the shade of a tent, calmly awaiting our arrival. When he heard of the petrol disaster he chuckled with amusement and poured us some tea. There was a young boy there, he said, with a motor scooter. If we offered him a fair price it was likely he would scoot back to Agades with an empty petrol can, have it filled and bring it back within the space of a couple of hours. The youth was found and named his price: an English shirt. Terms agreed, he jumped onto his scooter, revved up and accel- erated away leaving us all spluttering in a great cloud of dust. All we could do was wait, so we lazed in the tent with Rhossi's family, watching his wife make a kind of rancid butter. The creamy camel milk, first skimmed from a brimming gourd, had been poured into a goatskin which was now being methodically pounded and manipu- lated, evidently to curdle the contents – a very lengthy business. With the Tuareg, milk is never wasted; if not consumed at once, butter, cheese and soured milk are made from it, but when it is in really plentiful supply they can exist on it for weeks at a time, without any water to supplement their diet at all. Rhossi was very happy to play with his children, an endearing trait common to all Tuareg fathers. The children of the Tuareg, like those of other primitive peoples, are unusually trouble-free; they fend for themselves from an early age, learning how to accept hunger, thirst, heat and cold without complaint. It is rare for them to squabble, fight or hurt one another and even rarer for them to disobey their parents, and yet they don't lack spirit. When good things come their way, they are automatically shared equally amongst them, never grabbed greedily. The dignity of the Tuareg men and women alike – which never leaves them – naturally rubs off on their offspring.

For the first few years of their lives the boys and girls are treated much the same, their days consisting of a balance between certain responsibilities gradually undertaken – such as gathering wood, carrying babies on their backs, and minding goats – and freedom to amuse themselves. The games they play are simply variations of the games played the world over: hop-scotch, five-stones, tag, and so on, all of which adapt to the environment. They wear scant clothing if any, and the boys' hair is shaved but for a tuft on the crown of the head, said to be the means by which he would be carried to heaven if he died in infancy. As they grow up, the boys begin to participate in their fathers' activities, learning all about the camels, and even accompanying them on certain journeys. Whenever boys are allowed to join the men, they are expected to do all and any menial tasks, so that they learn how to work and how to endure protracted periods of hardship and discomfort. Meanwhile the girls are acquiring all their mothers' skills which are confined to the home, and to the head. The women are the more educated sex in the Tuareg society, being better versed in reading and writing, and responsible for teaching the children. Boys only learn up until the point when other activities make such demands on them that they haven't time, but girls continue to learn throughout their adolescence. At the age of about sixteen a boy takes on the veil, and thereafter he is classified as a man.

During the time we were waiting with Rhossi for the boy on the scooter to return with the petrol, a man came into the camp from out of the sparse desert with a tiny cheetah kitten on the end of a string. He had found it, he said, abandoned by its mother. It was very young and defenceless, wide-eyed and trembling with fear. The man was taking it to the market at Agades to sell. Unable to resist it, yet quite aware of all the impracticalities of owning a wild animal in our rootless circumstances, we bought it from him. Our idea was to rear it until it could at least look after itself in the face of danger, and then let it return once more to its natural habitat. About the size of an average domestic cat, the kitten was light and bony to handle, though its lean form was disguised in a fluff of soft yellow fur, through which pale cream stripes ran down from its spine. In the Landrover it leapt for the cover of the back seats and hid, in terror of all those human faces. The Tuareg said we were crazy to buy a useless animal, but agreed that it wouldn't live if left to its own devices. That the man who found it should put a price on it seemed to them a very silly move, and not wholly commendable. Within a few days the cheetah had grown accustomed to us and let us stroke its soft back and ears with its eyes half-closed. If a stranger approached, its hair stood on end all over its body and its claws extended viciously as it arched its back. If the stranger still advanced it would curl its lips and let out a warning hiss from the back of its throat – very alarming from so small a creature, and not to be ignored by anyone. As it grew more confident, it ate more hungrily, so that by the time we had to part with it its body had doubled in weight and it was sleek and alert. We gave it to the owner of the garden in Agades to look after, as he had a pup the same age. The cheetah and pup grew up alongside one another, tumbling and playing like brothers, eating from one bowl and coiled up together in sleep. It was ten months before we were to see it again, by which time it had grown to almost full size and was a healthy, powerful animal. It still played with the dog, but it was less gentle with other animals and people. Not many weeks later, we heard that it had had to be turned back into the wild, the best place for it.

At length the buzz of the scooter motor was heard and the haze of dust that came with it appeared over the horizon. We were able to fill up with petrol, and in the end one shirt seemed a low price to pay for such an enjoyable afternoon.

The first time we returned to Agades after our marriage, Rhossi – who had known us both before we knew each other – was so pleased about it that he said he would throw a party for us at his village, to celebrate the occasion in the Tuareg tradition. We were naturally very touched, and delighted to have an excuse to go to his village again. At that time of year, the community was still at Kourboubou, but Rhossi said that the pasture was poor and the animals scattered far and wide. He proposed, therefore, to buy two sheep in the market, as long as we could transport them to the village where they would be slaughtered and prepared for the *mechoui* – spit-roasting over a charcoal fire. He planned the party for three days hence, so we decided to take the two sheep out there the next day. This proved to be quite a performance. The sheep didn't like travelling by vehicle and it upset their stomachs dreadfully. So thankful were we to arrive that we did not notice the lack of people in the tent and grass-house village. We unloaded the sheep, tethered them and set to cleaning up the evil smelling mess from the interior of the vehicle, and then began to wonder where everyone was. In amongst the maze of dry and thorny trees that concealed the village, we knew there was a well of some importance, and now began to walk towards it in the hope of finding everyone there. Wells in the Sahara tend to be a vital nerve centre, particularly for communication between the nomads, as at one time or another they are bound to meet one another there. Thus, they have developed into the focal point of social contact. We were not to be disappointed: even before we came within sight of the well we heard the clamour of activity and the slosh of water. The wells are often – like this one – encircled by a concrete ramp that slopes down to a great circular trough. The men stand in the centre pulling up buckets of water and throwing them briskly onto the sloping table of smooth concrete. The livestock, controlled by more men and boys, stand at the trough drinking their fill. The mere sight of so much water being thrown about fills the heart of the parched, water-deprived nomad with a thrill of happiness, and the atmosphere around a busy well is always one of gaiety.

In recent times the Niger government has made valiant attempts to 'centralize' the nomads of the mountains by digging more wells and encouraging them to settle their encampments around them. It was thought that in this way the government could control the activities of the pastoral population, building schools and health centres to organize the society towards urbanization. The nomads were delighted by the new wells which at once made life easier for them, but apart from that nothing has changed: they continue to come and go like the shadow of a bird, to no-one knows just where.

The animals of the wandering nomad always seem to know when they are approaching a well. Barely perceptibly the pace quickens, and then the goats that have been straggling behind to feed en route start to bound towards the head of the group. As the well comes into view they charge forward, goats leaping, sheep jostling, and donkeys trotting nimbly. The camels are normally held back by men, but on arrival are given priority. The vegetation around the well is usually greener and more succulent than elsewhere, so once the animals are watered they are given a chance to graze while the people fill their *gerbers* with water, ready to sling on the donkeys and camels for carrying back to the camp. Sometimes, when the day is particularly fine, the women will wash clothes, laying their voluminous garments out flat on the concrete and rubbing them with soft stone, or even with a block of soap if they are lucky, then draping them over the prickly thorn trees to dry. The happy sounds of high-pitched laughter and shouted conversations are more or less indistinguishable from those made by any group of women, anywhere in the world. They all, men and women equally, take advantage of the occasion by washing themselves and their children, limiting their personal washing to their heads and arms, but dowsing the little ones from head to foot. It is quickly apparent that the children of the Tuareg are fairer skinned than their parents, and it has been suggested that this is because they are more frequently washed. This is not very convincing since it is such a general situation, and the adults are by no means unclean. Fortunately, the lack of humidity in the Saharan air is conducive to cleaner bodies, as perspiration dries before it has a chance to become stale or to infect the clothing. This clean, dry atmosphere also discourages the spread of diseases and viruses in the Saharan people, the most serious ailments being restricted to malnutrition, and to a diminishing amount of malaria, though of course such complaints as eye disorders and certain skin diseases are apparent amongst them all.

When we had at last found Rhossi's brother in the throng of people around the crowded well, we were told that Rhossi had gone to visit a neighbouring encampment to tell them of our fête, and that we were to leave the two sheep tethered under a tree in the Kourboubou encampment. It is customary to inform all the neighbouring nomads when a celebration is planned, so that they can all come over on their camels and take part. It is, so we were told, most important to have as many Tuareg as possible at such an occasion. Returning to the village we found the sheep already tethered in the shade and two men engaged in digging a shallow pit in the sand. They explained that in this they were going to build a fire, well in advance of the time to start cooking, so that it could burn slowly, increasing in temperature, until the sheep's carcases were ready to be suspended over the by-then red-hot glow of the embers.

On the day of the fête, Rhossi came up to us in Agades to tell us to take some warm clothes as we would probably be up all night. He wanted us to arrive in the early afternoon. Luckily, although it was very hot, it was a calm and clear day without a cloud to interrupt the dense blueness of the sky. Once more branching off the road to weave our way through the thorny trees to Kourboubou, we were struck by a sense of excited anticipation. Parking in the shade, we wandered into the clearing and saw at once that the same two men were now bending over the fiery sand pit, raking and poking the charcoal in a shimmer of heat. Two stakes had now been driven into the ground at each end of the pit, and the carcasses of the sheep – with thin poles driven through their bodies from head to tail – were balanced on top. As we walked over we could smell the unfamiliar aroma of roasting meat, seasoned with pepper and salt and chili powder. The men were stripped to the waist as the heat was intense, but not once did they cease to turn the skewered mutton so that the best results could be attained.

In the clearing a large tent had been erected, its leather canopy casting a dense dark shadow through which no rays of sunlight permeated. On the sandy floor of the tent, striped rugs of brilliant colours had been laid. Rhossi came over to us and, chuckling warmly, he led us by the hands to the tent where we all sat, thankfully drinking in the coolness of the deep shade. He was looking fine in a crisp blue *gandoura* with white silk embroidery, and he had evidently spent a little longer than his usual fifteen seconds in arranging his *taguelmoust*. After admiring his robes, his new sandals and his scent (Tuareg men and women often wear perfumed oils on their skin for special occasions and amongst the men it is considered in no way effeminate), we were joined by two of his brothers, and another man. Once they had all stepped out of their sandals, greeted us and seated themselves on the rugs, a very low wooden table – more like a round tray with legs – was uncovered in the back of the tent, revealing all the necessities for making tea, including a neat bundle of kindling to start a fire. The friend – who became nicknamed *Eh Le Suan Shahi* (He Who Makes the Tea) because he was so adept at it – settled himself comfortably at the front of the tent, and scooped a shallow basin in the sand with his forearm, in which to settle the fire. Within minutes he had a brisk blaze dancing and the kettle steaming and rattling its lid. After an exaggerated performance of pouring the tea from a height of several feet, to aerate the tea and produce a momentary head of bubbles at the brim of the small glass, giving rise to much pleasure, we were at last allowed to drink some of it. The men all chattered amicably and toasted us every few minutes, whenever they remembered why we were there, whereupon we toasted their absent friends, they toasted our relatives, we toasted their children, and so it went on, each phrase reiterated on the arrival of every newcomer, until it had become a huge joke and everyone was helpless with laughter. At least a couple

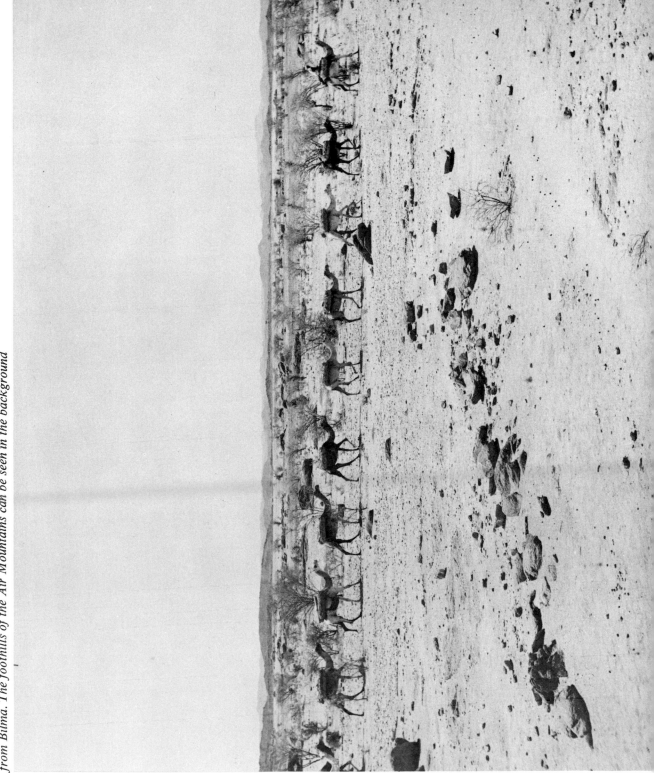

A camel caravan passes through the scrub desert towards Agades, laden with pillars of salt from Bilma. The foothills of the Aïr Mountains can be seen in the background

A corner of the busy market square at Agades. A woman carries a baby on her back, as well as a bundle of grass and a roll of matting. Beneath the shabby stalls clay water-vessels and basket work can be seen The dried dates in the foreground are sold by the handful.

A Targui of the Aïr Mountains, wearing good examples of the leather pouches and wallets common to all Tuareg. Some are used as containers for things like snuff, while others have excerpts from the Koran stitched inside, and are worn to ward off evil spirits

A Targui of the Aïr Mountains tends a charcoal fire that roasts the meat skewered above it

of hours had passed in this relaxed and contented frame of mind, when we decided to wander about the encampment. Soon we found ourselves amidst the sprawled group of woven-mat huts that constituted the village, where the village life was peacefully continuing: young women were pounding millet, and the even thuds as the pestle hit the bottom of the mortar, and the bleat of a young kid were the only sounds but for the buzz of flies. Older women sat in the shade of the grass houses and tents on rudimentary beds, constructed like a low sloping platform from carved poles supported at either end and covered by a rigid mat. According to the wealth or status of the family, the simple furniture is more or less finely carved, though in the poorer families there is no furniture at all. Apart from a bed, the other common item is a Y-shaped piece of wood some four or five feet high, embedded in the ground and used to hang things from; in some cases this again is carved and polished. In the larger dwellings there are usually two of these, with another pole horizontally balanced between them in the forks of the Ys.

As we wandered amongst the people, greeting them in the desultory afternoon atmosphere, one by one different women approached us and asked us to have a look at their eye maladies. In most instances there was little we could do besides washing them, but they were particularly insistent with regard to the babies and very small children. No sooner had we settled ourselves with our medical chest under a thorn tree, than a long line of ailing people assembled. The only man was limping with pain. The skin on his feet, as with all Tuareg, was tough and thick from years of walking barefoot on rough ground. In fact, so insensitive and leathery are their feet that they can take a needle, or a long sharp thorn which is an effective substitute, and sew up their foot wounds without even feeling it. Around his heels, where the skin had cracked badly, it was in one spot septic and very swollen. We treated him as best we could, cleaning and disinfecting the area and giving him a knitted woollen sock to wear, together with a healing and moisturising ointment. He had been an easy patient, but the tiny babies were less good – squirming, wriggling and yelling, averting their faces instinctively from our wads of antiseptic cotton wool. Finally, after a long clinic session, everyone had been attended to, and we became swiftly aware that the afternoon was beginning to fade – and from the direction of the clearing, we could hear music.

We returned through the bushes and undergrowth to find a considerable gathering in the clearing that had been quite empty before. Small fires flickered here and there, and the women, decoratively dressed in black, blue and white, were all seated together in a dense circle under a tree. With the black shawls draped over their heads they resembled a flock of immobile ravens, with fingers for wing-tips, fluttering over the drums or clapping in time to its beat. There was a nucleus of ring-leaders, older women, who led the songs and whose voices could be heard above the rest, while all the others looked on with interest, cradling their babies and joining in the chorus with enthusiasm. The men were also dressed up in fine attire, their head-dresses impressive in their superbly sculptural arrangements, gleaming purple and inky-blue in the warmth of the descending sun, and their swords, worn rakishly, catching a flash of silver as they moved. Many of the men were still mounted on camels, but they were holding back their mounts in the obscurity of the thorn trees. There must have been over a hundred people present, and the clamour of human voices, the throb of the *tindi* and the spasmodic interjection of a camel's roar made the empty desert come alive. We were asked to return to the tent as the *mechoui* was ready to eat: as we approached we saw the two spit-roasters carrying the succulent meat over from the fire, now a furnace of heat. It was placed on a low table and about twelve of us seated ourselves cross-legged around it. The etiquette of these matters demands that you select the most delicious morsel you can find, rip it off with your fingers and offer it to your neighbour; in turn you accept every bit that is offered to you, and so the meal progresses. On repletion, the carcass is carried off, and a jug or bowl of fresh camel milk – still warm, thick and creamy – is passed around for everyone to enjoy. Then tea is made. Few meals can taste as good as this, especially to the Tuareg whose habitual diet is very monotonous by comparison.

Having eaten we turned our attention again to the singing. By now the sky was streaked with deep pink and opal clouds, behind which the sun had set. The singers were swelling in numbers, and a line of perhaps twenty of them had formed: chanting and clapping in unison, their silver jewellery sparkled and flashed. The men faced them in a group, and one by one, began to dance towards them. Feet stamping, bodies swaying, they shrieked in a crescendo of excitement, and began swirling around, all their clothes billowing about them. The women were erect, dignified and unbending – never faltering in the words of the songs, never losing the rhythm of the lead singer.

So engrossed were we in watching the performance that we had failed to see the approach of the camels. In perfect time to the music, camels were prancing into the midst of the activity, heads held well back by the riders to discipline their movements. We were astonished at the grace and control demonstrated by these large and ungainly beasts, but were even more surprised when they began a beauti-fully co-ordinated trot in a circle around the tree under which the women were grouped. There were half a dozen fine white Tibesti camels, and the circles started wide; as the music and singing became more earnest and piercing, the circles became smaller, until the camels were dancing their way statuesquely through the crowd of seated women. As we watched, one rider suddenly bent low and hoisted a baby of not more than a few months up onto the camel from the arms of its mother. All the crowd cheered and laughed, while the camel and rider continued their circuitous route through the crowd. It soon emerged that the man was the father of the child, and was showing off his capability in the saddle, to everyone's delight.

The next thing we were aware of was a great gangling camel, charging across the clearing at terrific speed; its rider was a young boy, not even veiled yet, on whose face horror was imprinted. The camel fled towards the undergrowth and crashed against the sharp thorn trees in its haste. At once an older man took up the chase, followed by others. It was some minutes before they returned, and the crowded clearing was in silence by the time the boy's camel was led back in. The boy was lying across the knees of another rider, who rode gently through the clearing towards the village centre. The man on foot leading the now passive camel came directly to us and asked us to go at once to the boy to treat his wounds. Evidently the reign on the camel had snapped, and the boy was too inexperienced to control such a large beast. It had stampeded in panic and the boy had been thrown to the ground. When we saw him we knew he would be all right. He had had concussion and had grazed his shin and ankle, but by the time these were bandaged he had quite recovered his composure. Nevertheless for a boy of his age to be subjected to such a public exhibition was a grave humiliation, and would be remembered critically for years to come.

The whisper had gone around straight away that he was unhurt, and the festivities were resumed at an even greater pitch. After the baby had been snatched – a symbol of the bond between the rider and the woman – other young men began the traditional courtship with the girls. Watching a seated girl under the tree, a young man steers his camel directly towards her as though to trample her, veering away at the last second. She admires his prowess, but does not necessarily approve his having selected her. By a sign she will indicate whether she welcomes his attentions, and if so the flirtation becomes more serious. If not, he will at once transfer them to another girl, or resignedly not attempt to flirt with anyone. In the normal run of events, the Tuareg communities have a special evening celebration from time to time, called an *ahal*, at which all are present, but which is specifically intended for the girls to recite love poems that they have composed themselves, and sing songs filled with sentiment, and for the boys to make advances towards the girls. The girl has her own power in that she is free to reject any boy, or even to accept him and reject him later. A courting couple is free to wander away alone without risking the disapproval of their elders, and a degree of intimacy will normally take place, although sexual intercourse is rare in pre-marital relationships. An illegitimate baby is regarded as a very serious wrong-doing, and its mother is immediately cast out of the society, or relegated to the most humble and lowly status. Although there is no statistical proof, it is supposed that in the main babies born out of wedlock are disposed of at birth to lessen the embarrassment of the mother, and to spare the child an ignominy that it would bear all its life.

During the parade of camels, which was enacted with increasing spirit and enthusiasm, the camels prancing in a rapid, jaunty movement like circus horses in the ring, we were incredulous to see yet another extension of their versatility: we were seated outside the tent, facing an evening sky in front of which the crooked twigs of the thorn trees were blackly silhouetted. The sand of the clearing appeared violet in colour in the transitory twilight, and the horizon was dotted with groups of camels and riders fast approaching the loud and teeming gathering. The entire desert area was a mass of Tuareg, camels and music. The shrieks of men could be heard over the haunting chant of female voices, a chant that seemed to linger in the air like an echo even after the song had finished. From the direction of the village on our right, we were suddenly conscious of four unusually imposing camels nearing our tent: the riders were formidable in their dark costumes and very erect posture, and their camels stepped high, in exact time with one another. The women on our left at once stopped their song and broke into a familiar and rousing tune, originally associated with the overtures to a dangerous battle. Tuareg women have been renowned through history for the aid and encouragement they have given their menfolk in times of war; on one memorable occasion they even formed the front line together with their children to conceal the men, as the whole company moved towards the enemy, knowing that it would be a cruel opponent indeed who was prepared to slaughter women and children for the sake of battle. There are innumerable small instances of the courage and selflessness of the Tuareg women under desperate circumstances or dire need. Now as the chorus grew in fervour and emotion, so the camels and their riders drew to a timely halt before us; then, in unison, with peculiarly guttural mutterings from the riders, they seemed as though about to kneel. Having lowered themselves onto their fore-knees, however, they stopped at that; and with their hind legs still fully extended, a strange dance began. Riders had to lean back to maintain their balance, and so were almost in a straight and standing position, feet on camels' necks while the camels' heads were wrenched back, their aloof and disdainful expressions exaggerated in this position. So remarkable was this feat of the four camels dancing forwards and round in circles on their knees, that we could hardly believe our eyes. Together, without any outward sign passing between them, the riders suddenly changed their utterances into a powerful cry, and the camels raised themselves back up onto all-fours, and stood stock still as if turned to stone. Seconds later, four more camels reached them and one of the earlier dances began, until the first four trotted off in single file and the second four started to repeat the triumphant dance on their knees. The strain on both camels and riders was obviously intense; on standing again both trembled a little and breathed heavily, which we were able to observe as they performed at such close proximity to us. At the end of this demonstration we were quite speechless with wonder, and felt both honoured and privileged to have been the object of such a memorable and moving show of skill. For us this was the climax of the event, though for the Tuareg participating it clearly marked the beginning of a night of festive entertainment, to which more and more Tuareg, singly and in small groups, continued to arrive.

By now the night was black and only the spark of fires everywhere indicated the many groups of people. It was November, when however hot the day may be there is a dramatic chilling in the temperature as the sun sets, and invariably a cold night ensues; but no-one was aware of the cold, only of the excitement and the unfamiliar throngs of people in the normally sparse and empty desert terrain. The sounds of *tindi* and *imzad* – a one-stringed violin based on half of a hollow gourd that makes a sorrowful, wailing sound – floated through the night to spasmodic bursts of singing and dancing. The newcomers mingled with the others, all from different camps, and all delighting in the opportunity to meet one another. As the camels swept past on the periphery of a group, all the young men and boys watched the rider closely; equally, when a young rider was in the saddle and went through the

Three Tuareg seated outside a typical nomadic Tuareg dwelling of the Aïr Mountains, woven grass mats, cloth and leather stretched over a bent wooden frame

Rhossi's brother: a typical nomadic Tuareg of the Aïr Mountains, wearing the indigo-dyed taguelmoust *that leaves a blue tinge on the skin, giving rise to the name 'the Blue Men'*

Tuareg women and children participating in a music and singing festival at Kourboubou. One woman uses a hollow gourd upturned in a wooden bowl as a drumming instrument. The heavy silver ear-rings are typical of the region

A Targui at Kourboubou with a large white Tibesti camel, branded on the neck, held on a close rein for dancing in time to the music. The long leather fringes attached to the saddle discourage flies from settling on the camel

clearing, the older men scrutinized his carriage, his balance and his composure as well as the movements of the camel. We were reminded of a different festival at which we chanced to be present. Approaching Agades from the borders of Nigeria in the south, we had reached a village of considerable size called Abalak, situated between Tahoua and In-Gall, where a Peulh festival was taking place. There was a vast majority of Peulh people, but the handful of Tuareg on camels were conspicuous even in such a crowd. The Peulh or Fulani history and way of life could form the basis of another book, but what impressed us at this festival was the way in which the Tuareg seemed to dominate over the mass of Peulh people, stalking proudly amongst them on their tall camels, commanding remarkable authority. They carried riding canes of twisted leather thonging which swished in the air as they brandished them, and they were clearly relishing their position of superiority. Now, at Kourbou-bou, each had to work much harder at making any sort of impact; riders, dancers, singers and musicians alike were all trying their best to be noticed and to receive the admiring glances that mean so much in their terms. We wandered amongst them, and were glad that, as the only Europeans present, we were able to attract little attention, but simply to enjoy their festivities.

It was late when everyone began to settle down for the night; the moon had risen at last and cast its cold light over the pale desert environment, as we wrapped ourselves as warmly as possible in extra clothes and local blankets, and lay down in the sand to sleep. As we lay amongst the dozens of weary Tuareg we were still too full of the impressions of the evening to drift into sleep, and instead lay wondering about the future of these people around us. With so little on their side, it is almost inconceivable that they can hope to survive without undergoing radical changes in their way of life, or without having to make major compromises. Every year, as the Saharan drought persists, the very tenuous nature of the nomads' present existence is underlined in harsh and unavoidable terms. But the drought – with all the suffering and misery it entails – cannot be blamed entirely for the disintegration of their lifestyle. Such traditional occasions as this festival at Kourboubou are so easy to debase and commercialize when exposed to the ruthless and single-minded treatment of the westernized tour operator, who will pay to make the Tuareg perform, but who is really paying them to surrender their spontaneity, individuality, and even their integrity. Thus an alien economy begins to dictate to them, and they embark upon the long and downhill path towards 'civilization' and conformity.

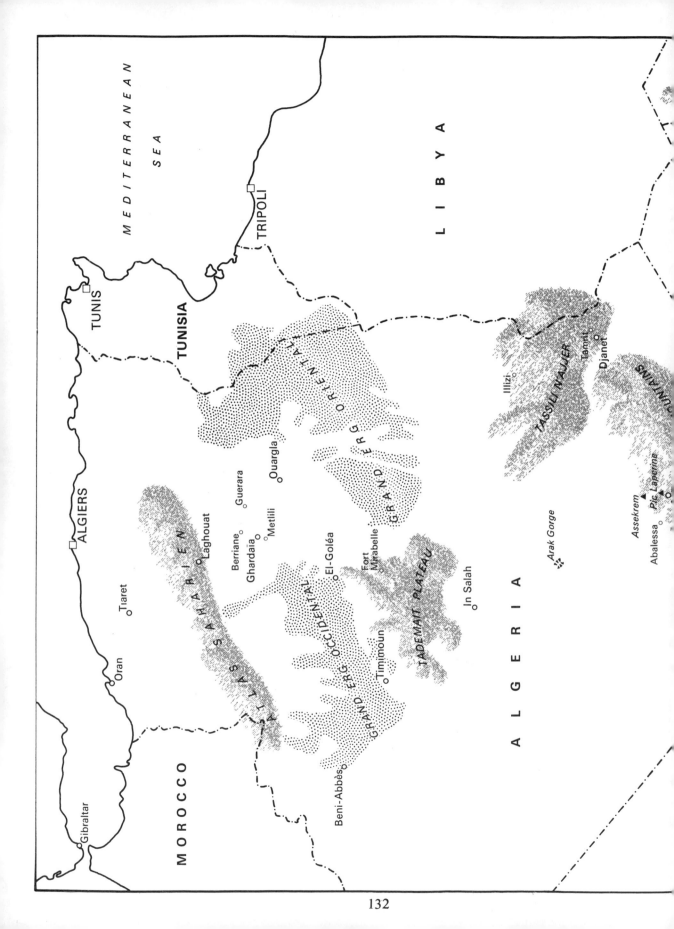

MEDITERRANEAN SEA

LIBYA

TUNISIA

TRIPOLI

TUNIS

ALGIERS

MOROCCO

ALGERIA

GRAND ERG ORIENTAL

GRAND ERG OCCIDENTAL

SAHARAN ATLAS

TADEMAIT PLATEAU

TASSILI NAJJER

Illizi

Tamrit
Djanet

Assekrem
Abalessa
Pic Laperine

Arak Gorge

In Salah

Fort Mirabelle

El-Goléa

Timimoun

Beni-Abbès

Ouargla

Guerara
Metlili
Berriane
Ghardaïa
Laghouat

Tiaret

Oran

Gibraltar

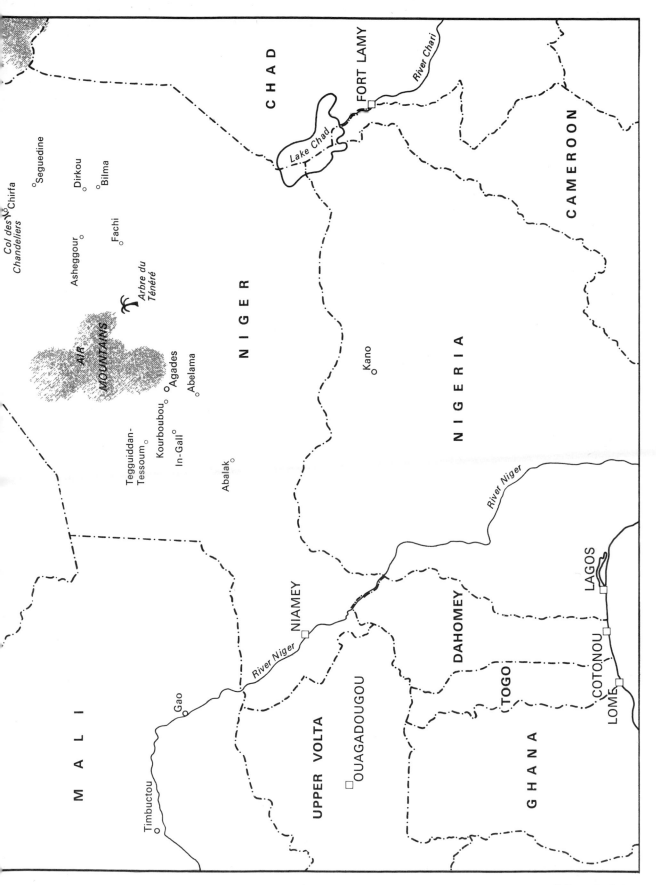

CHAD

FORT LAMY

River Chari

CAMEROON

Lake Chad

Seguedine

Dirkou

Bilma

Col des
Chandeliers

Chirfa

Fachi

Asheggour

Arbre du
Ténéré

NIGER

AIR
MOUNTAINS

Agades

Abelama

Kano

NIGERIA

Kourboubou

Tegguiddan-
Tessoum

In-Gall

Abalak

River Niger

LAGOS

NIAMEY

River Niger

DAHOMEY

COTONOU

Gao

TOGO

LOMÉ

MALI

UPPER VOLTA

OUAGADOUGOU

GHANA

Timbuctou

133

© Gentry Books Ltd.

Glossary

ahal: romantic Tuareg evening celebration
Amenokal: chief of a Tuareg confederation
burnous: woollen cloak with hood
chebka: broken rock desert comprising 'network' of stones
chorba: clear soup with noodles and spices
cous-cous: rolled and steamed semolina dish served with vegetable sauce
djellaba: woollen overgarment
erg: sand desert
gandoura: loose robe of light material
gerber: goatskin container
guelta: water pool
imzad: one-stringed violin
Inadin: Tuareg silver smiths
Muezzin: holy man who calls out the prayers from the minaret of a mosque
oued: dried-up river-bed, that still flows from time to time
reg: stony, rocky desert
taguelmoust: veil worn by Tuareg men
tamarshak: the Tuareg language
Targui: a Tuareg man
Targuia: a Tuareg woman
tassili: plateau
ténéré: desert
tifinagh: the Tuareg script
tindi: wooden skin-covered drum
wadi: dried-up river bed
zeriba: hut made from palm fronds or grass

Index

Index

Numerals in **bold** type refer to illustrations.

Daïa, legend of, 8
desert: accidents in, 31-2, 61, 99, 100-2,
    111, 112-13; caravan routes across, 9,
    17-18, 96, 105, 107; *chebka*, 8; climatic
    change in, 49-50, 50-5; cultivated crops
    in, 9, 82-5, 102-3; difficulties of
    travelling in, 1, 16, 17, 36, 39, 55,
    67, 72, 80-2, 99;
    effects of goats on vegetation of, 31;
    encroachment of, 14, 17; need for
    guides in, 100, 101, 102, 111;
    irrigation of, 10-11, 83-4;
    motorized transport in, 13, 15-16, 17, 18,
    99, 102; rainfall in, 8, 31, 80, 95;
    reg, 13; storm in, 60-1; trees in, 14, 34,
    f.40, 49-50, 58, 111-12; vegetation in, 1,
    8, 14, 18, 36, 50-5, 80-1, 82, 98-9,
    112, 117; wildlife in, 36-7, 55, 67, 68,
    73, 99-100, 110, 114, 115-16.
    See also drought
desert roses, 15-16
Dictionary of Tamarshak, Charles de
    Foucauld, 33
Dirkou, 101, 109
Djado, **f. 64,** 109
Djanet, 39, 49, 55, 57, 62, 74, 111
Djerma people, 96, 105
dogs, 35, 40, 58, 112
donkeys, 10, 36, 58, 59, 60, 117
drought, 19, 30-1, 35, 46, 95, 113, 131
drums, 10, 43, 44, 65. *See also tindi*

El Aghouat, *see* Laghouat
El-Atteuf, 8
El-Goléa, 13, 14-17, **f.16,** 39
Elmiki, **f. 96,** 98
Europeans, 10, 13, 34, 102, 103, 111.
    See also tourists

Fachi, **f.97,** 106-7, 109, 111
'Fakir', Tuareg chief, 82-5
Fête de L'Aide, 59, 62-5
Fête de Tapis du M'zab, 9
fish, 37, 55, 56
flutes, 2, 3, 44, 45
Fort Mirabelle, 17
Foucauld, Charles de, 15, 32-4
French Camel Corps, 11, 105, 106
French Foreign Legion forts, 14, 16, 17,
    109. *See also* Algeria, French rule of
Fulani people, *see* Peulh people

Gao, 1
gazelle, Dorcas, 99, 112
Ghardaïa, 8-11, 12-13
Ghati camels, *see* camels
giraffe, 1, 55
goats: 56, 60, 117; effect on vegetation, 31;
    skins for *gerbers*, 63; for food, 63;
    sacrificial, 59, 63
Grand Erg Occidental, 14
grouse, Senegal, 100
gueltas, water pools, 32, 36, 49, 55, 56,
    58, 59, 66, 72
Guerara, 8
guinea fowl, helmeted, 100

'Hammah', Tuareg chief, 69, 70, 71-2, 73-4,
    75
Hausa people, 7, 95, 96, 97, 98, 105,
    109
Hoggar Mountains, 7, 17, 18, 19, 23-46
    passim, 49
Hoggar, Guardians of the, 35
hospitals: Agades, 102; Djanet, 69;
    El-Goléa, 15; Tamanrasset, 40, 41-2
hotels: Agades, 102; Djanet, 39;
    El-Goléa, 16; Ghardaïa, 13; Illizi, 91;
    In Salah, 17; Niamey, 97;
    Tamanrasset, 38, 39; Timimoun, 39.
    See also towns, development of; tourists

Ibadites, *see* Mozabite people
Illizi, 86-7
Inadin, Tuareg silver smiths, 30
In Gall, 131
In Gitane, 108
In Salah, 17-18
In Search of the Tassili Frescoes,
    Henri Lhote, 74
insects, 37, 79-80, 82-3, 85, 109
imzad, violin, 126
Istanbul, 98
Istanbul, Khalif of, 98
Italians, 34, 101-2. *See also*
    Europeans; tourists

Kano, 96
Koran, the, 12, 23, 62, 69.
    See also mosques, Moslem faith
Kourboubou, 114, 116, 117-31

Tibesti camels, *see* camels
Tibesti Mountains, 108
tifinagh, Tuareg script, 24, 36, 73
Timbuctou, 1, 18, 31
Timimoun, 17, 39
tindi, drum, **90,** 124, 126
Tin Hinan, Princess, legend of, 38-9
tin mining, **f.96,** 98
Tit, 19
Tit, Battle of, 11, 19
tourists, 1, 3, 13, 16, 19-20, 36, 49, 74, 79, 97, 99, 101-2, 106, 111, 131
towns, development of, 10, 12-13, 14, 16-17, 39
Trans-Saharan Highway, 7, 13, 16
Tribes of the Sahara, Lloyd Cabot Briggs, 95
Tuareg: and Amenokal, 29; and Arabs, 7, 23-4; and bread making, 65-6, 103-4; brotherliness of, 36, 106; and camels, 34-5, 60, 61-2, 65, 80, 81-2, 104-5, 107, 112, 117; and camel caravans, 105-6; camel saddles of, 108; and Chaamba, 7, 11, 16, 17; and childbirth, 103; children, 24-9, 40-2, 103, 115, 117, 125, 126-31; and Christian faith, 23, 32, 33; clan system of, 29; courtship ceremonies, 125; and cultivation of crops, 83-4, 102-3; dancing, 2-3, **f.32,** 43-5, 98, 124, 125-6, **130,** 131; dependence on livestock, 30, 35, 60, 61, 113; diet of, 62-3, 66, 67, 73, 114-15, 124; and disease, injuries, 40-2, 66, 68, 69-71, 117, 123; and divorce, 29; and dogs, 75-6; dress of, 18, 24, 30, 38, 57, 62, 102-3, 118, 123; and drought, 19, 30-1, 35, 46, 95, 113, 131; engagement ceremony, 64; fatalism of, 19, 35, 41, 69, 71, 113; fêtes of, **f.32,** 39, **52,** 59, 62-5, **76,** 116, 117-30, **130;** and French rule, 11, 33-4, 105; furniture of, 123; and *gerbers* from goat skins, 63; greeting ceremony of, 56, 58; as guides across desert, 55, 100, 101, 102; and Hausa, 7, 95, 96; hierarchical society of, 29-30, 83, 84; honesty of, 36-7; *Inadin*, silver smiths, 30; inheritance of wealth, status, 24-9, 98; and interment of dead, 71; jewellery, 62, 69, 91, **f.96, 129;**

legend of, 38-9; lifestyle when crossing desert, 55-6, 67-8, 106, 107; and marriage, 29; Meddak clan, 68, 69, 72; and traditional medicine, 30, 67, 68-9, 103, 107; attitude to modern medicine, 40, 41, 42, 69, 103; and Moslem faith, 23-9, 59, 62, 73; music of, 2-3, 43-6, 64-5, 98, 123-4, 125-31; nomadic camps of, 34, **51,** 58-61, 65-6, 69-71, 73-5, **87, 127;** and Peulh, 7, 95, 131; physical appearance of, 18, 38, 44, 83; preparation of food, 34, 61, 62-3, 65-6, 67, 103-4, 114-15, 117-18, **122;** proverbs of, 29, 107; and raiding, 11, 18, 29, 30, 105; and rope making, 63; and slaves, 29-30, 83, 84; songs of, 64, 124, 126; spoken language of, *tamarshak,* 24, 33, 56; status of women, 24; and *taguelmoust,* 24, **25,** 30, 38, 44, 57, 84, 115, **128;** and tea drinking, 55-6, 59, 82-3, 118; and Tebu, 7, 95, 107, 109; and tourists, 19-20, 36, 74, 106, 131; in towns, 23, 38, 46, 91, 98; threats to independence of, 19-20, 31, 35, 46, 95, 103, 113, 131; and tracking, 56-7, 58, 82; and trade, 96, 104-5, 105-6; villages, sedentary encampments of, 19, 39-41, 82-5, 96, **f.112,** 114-16, 116-23; and wives, number of, 24, 69; in wars, 11, 16, 23-4, 30, 98, 126; women, 24, 29, 57, 83, 103, 115, 125; written language of, *tifinagh,* 24, 36, 73
Tuat, 17. *See also* In Salah
Turkish baths, 15

United States Air Force, 113
United States Government, 113

vipers, 17, 67, 73
vultures, Egyptian, 100

wells: 14, **f.40, f.56,** 83, 84; Asheggour, 101; Ghardaïa, 9; Kourboubou, 116-17; Ténéré, 111
White Sisters, *Soeurs Blanches,* 15, 41

xylophones, 1, 2, 43

zoos: Agades, 97; Niamey, 97